FRANCIS

*

A Saint's Way

JAMES COWAN

Author of the Acclaimed Bestseller
A Mapmaker's Dream

Liguori/Triumph
LIGUORI, MISSOURI

For Colin Beard,
lumen

✳

Published by Liguori/Triumph
An Imprint of Liguori Publications
Liguori, Missouri
www.liguori.org
www.catholicbooksonline.com

Library of Congress Cataloging-in-Publication Data

Cowan, James, 1942–
    Francis : a saint's way / James Cowan. — 1st ed.
       p. cm.
    Includes bibliographical references.
    ISBN 0-7648-0707-2
    1. Francis, of Assisi, Saint, 1182–1226. 2. Christian saints—Italy—Assisi—Biography. I. Title.

BX4700.F6 C69 2001
271'.302—dc21   00–052012

Contents

Introduction

How does one approach the life of a long-dead saint whose influence upon Catholics and non-Catholics alike has been so strong these past eight hundred years? Clearly, with difficulty. Francis is no ordinary saint, even within the Catholic pantheon. He stands as a unique figure whose behavior and personality set him apart from his fellow saints. These holy men and women conform to a type that we see as specifically religious, and their contribution to Christianity is easily recognizable. I'm thinking of the great scholar saints in particular—men such as Saint Augustine, Saint Bernard, Saint Benedict, Saint Thomas Aquinas, and Saint Bonaventure. These men, like their female counterparts Saint Teresa of Ávila and Saint Catherine of Siena, enhanced and invigorated the Christian tradition through their writings and monastic fervor. They were warriors of the Faith, not vagabonds.

Francis followed a different path. By choosing the road rather than the monastery as his principal place of abode, he made it acceptable for ordinary folk to live a spiritually committed life in the world. No longer did a man or woman have to retreat to a monastery in order to realize the Christian life; now they could practice an asceticism of the spirit in the context of normal everyday existence. Francis made it possible for people to live such a life outside the religious structures and institutions of his time. He was a preacher first before he was a contemplative. He was an enthusiast for life before he was a mystic. He understood that man's deepest desire was to have a relationship with God that was genuine and unhindered. Like the earliest of primitive peoples, Francis intuitively understood that any cult figure, any focus of religious devotion, should embody spirit before it embodied doctrine. In Francis's eyes, Christ—though not a cult figure—must have exemplified the primacy of spirit over doctrine.

I think this is the reason why I wanted to explore his life. Francis stood for something that was non-doctrinal and free. He had carved his spirituality out of the rock of his own existence. It was not something that was bestowed upon him amid the tranquillity of monastic routine or by some intimate act of grace. Unlike the scholar saints, he forged his own reality out of a lifelong confrontation with poverty. This was his talisman, his instrument of penitence. No one before him or since has remained as faithful as he to the principle of poverty as a spiritual discipline. He alone has made the act of dispossession into a virtue. The long tradition in defense of the reality of things that went as far back as the atomist philosophers of early Greece was once again being questioned. Francis recognized that ownership and the so-called "tyranny of things" constituted a barrier between himself and the freedom of the spirit.

In this age of affluence his testimony strikes a chord. Francis might have understood better than most the conflicts we all face in our bid to free ourselves from the tyranny of things. Modern technology, as we all know, is fast enveloping us in a maelstrom of gadgets. We find ourselves surrounded by labor-saving devices that are meant to free us so that we might enjoy something more essential. To our cost, however, we have found that gadgetry has manacled us more than ever. We are further, rather than nearer, from living within the preserve of the spirit-filled, the simple godliness of existence. Try as we might, we find it almost impossible to release ourselves from the demands made by a life conditioned by things. Francis, on the other hand, recognized early that the hidden face of truth could only reveal itself to someone in concert with openness, with insecurity, and with trust. He knew, as few before him had known, that being released from the prison of possession enabled him to live a life of unconditional acceptance.

My decision to study him was made easier by the fact that I had chosen to live in Italy—and within easy reach of his beloved Umbria. Quite early in my stay I used to walk down to the monastery of Le Celle near Cortona to sit in the tiny chapel next to the cave where he had once slept. The monastery had an archaic feel about its buildings, as if the entire place had been hewn from the valley in which it is located. It reminded me of certain Aboriginal caves that I had visited in the Australian desert. It occurred to me too that Francis was no ordinary fellow, and that his sanctity was no ordinary acquisition. He had laid claim to it only after a great battle with himself. I suddenly realized that his attributes—his gaiety, bizarre behavior, and his habit of wandering from place to place—were the product of a mind attuned to an unusually high level of endurance of suffering. Francis's anguish was caused by the knowledge that he couldn't escape the proximity and persistence of God's call, so for the last twenty years of his life he was forced to stand on the edge and peer into the eyes of his Maker.

How can a man do it to himself? I asked. What is the advantage of living so close to God that the entire body begins to collapse? Why should one pursue a life of such ascetical pain that every fiber of one's being is strung out, as if on a rack? Why deny the body? These were the questions that came to me whenever I sat in the chapel beside Francis's grotto. I was being assailed by arguments that revoked the reality of his life simply because I couldn't come to terms with what he represented. Francis, I kept telling myself, you are an hysteric, a masochist. You have made asceticism into a palliative in order to appease your own disenchantment with life. Far from it being spiritual nourishment that you offer, I suspect it is life-denial that underpins your existence. But even as I asked such questions, and struggled to repudiate them with less than convincing answers, I began to realize that the man had *still* managed to escape the trap I had set for him. It was then that I knew that he was urging me to follow in his footsteps.

I decided to enter his world. His caves and grottos, the monasteries founded in his name, the forest paths that he had once walked, the paintings and frescoes inspired by his life, the great basilicas built after his death, the towns of Tuscany and Umbria— now imprinted with his memory—all these formed the man's imaginative terrain. It was up to me to visit these places and glean from them some flavor of his existence. I soon realized that the man I thought I knew had adopted another disguise altogether. He was no longer the pious ascetic, the whirligig saint who spoke to birds. These are only aspects of his populist image. What I came to know and respect was a man in full possession of his faculties, a man driven by inner furies, a man who finally had the courage to refashion his personality in the interest of overcoming the prison of his own self.

I realized also that I was dealing less with a medieval ascetic than I was with the precursor of a more inward sensibility. Francis had chosen to explore his own psyche in his bid to release the spirit within. Unlike his contemporaries, who accepted religiosity as a given, he sought to impose on himself something extra—to embody Christ as an existential reality rather than as something solely inspired by an event in history. His entire ministry sprang from a belief that human beings might transcend themselves through a principled act of denial. This belief represents an extraordinary and somewhat modern sentiment. As few before him had done, Francis understood the difference between the mask of persona and the authenticity of character, between social behavior and individual endeavor. He made the primacy of the spirit into an imperative rather than the object of doctrinal or ritual observation.

Francis was less a medieval pietist than he was a revolution-ary. He brought to Christianity recollections of its origins amid the harsh terrain of the Egyptian desert. Unfortunately what had occurred there in the early centuries of the Christian era had not survived the sea crossing to Europe. The fervor, the unmitigated love of Christ, the desire to emulate him in all his actions—these ideals had somehow been diluted in the more benign climate of European monastic life. Theology not meditation, doctrine not ascetic practice had become paramount as the new learning of the universities made its presence felt throughout Europe. Men were more content to argue a point of dogma than they were to go down on their knees in the presence of God. Knowledge and intellect had subsumed the humble rapprochement with the God that the early Desert Fathers felt was so important.

As a wandering ascetic, Francis saw his first task to be one of unblocking the well so that the spring might once more bubble forth. Intuitively, he knew that people needed to re-invest in the ancient tradition of asceticism if they were to bring to their lives any inkling of ecstatic experience. He understood more than most that materiality was inimical to the idea of going beyond ordi-nary limits. A man or woman must learn how to deny themselves if they were ever going to take responsibility for their inheritance as human beings marked by Adam's sin. For another thing, Francis may not have seen Heaven as being the most important aspect of man's hoped-for abode after death. He was more interested in man's existence in this world, in his ability to plumb the mystery of the Supreme Being, as the individual's rightful task. A man or woman must learn how to enter into the spirit of will-lessness if he or she were to enter the realm of the spirit. Whether this realm was called Heaven may have been less relevant to Francis; he sim-ply wanted people to accept the nature of their destiny: to be-come bearers of the sublime rather than mere vessels of earth.

Traveling about Umbria and Tuscany in his footsteps became

a pilgrimage for me. I soon found myself adopting his manner-
isms, and like him journeying with no fixed expectation in mind.
One day I might visit a monastery, another I might seek out a
fresco. Sometimes I would explore a ruin, at other times I might
tour a museum. I would sit in grottos and take notes, or gaze out
from monastery courtyards and think about his memory. He was
always on my mind. I tried to imagine how he might have re-
acted to a leper on the road, or what he thought about while he
was preaching his sermons. At every stage of my journey I attempted to put myself in his shoes so that I might experience a
little of his joy and anguish. It was a worthwhile experiment. I
soon discovered that I was changing, that I was becoming more
tolerant of Francis's eccentricities. I came to accept that the primitive nature of his soul was originary to Francis, rather than the
reflection of any lack of consciousness on his part. This man was
in league with the invisible, and with the great endeavor of humankind throughout history to cultivate the spirit. I admired him
for that. He had made it possible for me to assume my own
originary being once more, and so be guided homewards.

Sitting in the crypt in the lower church of the basilica of St.
Francis in Assisi one day, I knew that I had finally come home.
His body lay in its crypt above me. The bones of his closest friends,
Masseo, Rufino, Angelo, and Leo—not to mention those of that
mysterious Roman lady, Giocoma di Settisoli—lay entombed in
stone nearby. All of them were sleeping. All of them were dreaming the same dream of spiritual renewal and hope. The drama of
their lives was palpable that morning; I could feel their presence
in the lamp-lit stone vault that was their last resting place. I knew
then that the book I must write should in some way reflect the
excitement of their adventure. These people had taken unto themselves the inspiration of one man's life and turned it into a revolutionary mode of conduct for everyone. They had made poverty,
chastity, and obedience into escutcheons on a coat-of-arms fit

for soldiers like themselves, committed to defending their honor against the encroachments of materiality and indifference.

This book is not a complete history of Francis's life, but an attempt to enter into the spirit of the man. It is also an attempt to place him firmly in his time and to explore areas of his life that have not previously been dealt with in great depth. I am thinking particularly of the events at La Verna when he received the Stigmata, and his encounter with the sultan in Egypt. I see both these events as being linked, and that La Verna would not have happened without his visit to the Holy Land. After exploring the literature of the time I am firmly convinced that Francis was in some way mysticized by his experience at Damietta, talking as he did with the Egyptian sages at the sultan's court. From them he learned new techniques of inwardness that he was able to immediately put into practice on his return to Italy. One could say that after Damietta, Francis was a changed man. He abandoned his job as Minister General of his order and retired to a life of almost full-time meditation and prayer. La Verna was its fruit.

The book is also a celebration of a very intimate side of Italy— the Italy of the imagination. When one moves away from the grandiose works of art and architecture that make up this most blessed of countries, it's possible to find a land that still retains the ability to contemplate itself. For any thoughtful observer, such a land offers real opportunities to go beyond mere appearance and to experience what inspired so many religious figures of the past. Hopefully, this book will inspire others to make the pilgrimage to central Italy in pursuit of that elusive world in which great spirituals continue to fashion their own unique encounters with the mysteries of the spirit. If this invitation should be offered, then we must give thanks to one man, Francis.

JAMES COWAN
CORTONA, ITALY

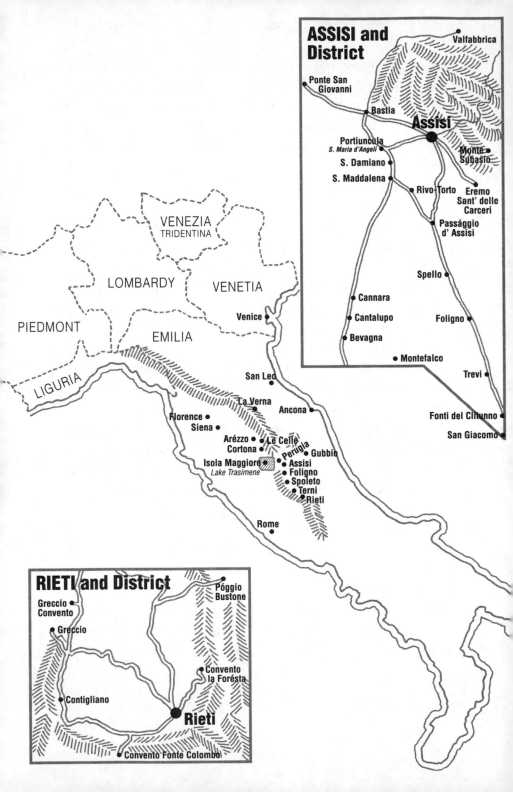

ASSISI and District

Valfabbrica

Ponte San Giovanni

Bastia

Assisi

Portiuncula
S. Maria d'Angeli

Monte Subasio

S. Damiano

S. Maddalena

Rivo-Torto

Eremo Sant' delle Carceri

Passággio d' Assisi

Spello

Cannara

Cantalupo

Foligno

Bevagna

Montefalco

Trevi

Fonti del Clitunno

San Giacomo

VENEZIA
TRIDENTINA

LOMBARDY

VENETIA

PIEDMONT

EMILIA

Venice

LIGURIA

San Leo

La Verna

Ancona

Florence

Siena

Arézzo

Le Celle

Cortona

Perugia

Gubbio

Isola Maggiore
Lake Trasimene

Assisi

Foligno

Spoleto

Terni

Rieti

Rome

RIETI and District

Póggio Bustone

Greccio Convento

Greccio

Convento la Forésta

Contigliano

Rieti

Convento Fonte Colombo

CHAPTER ONE

On a Mountain
in Tuscany

✳

I t was a chilly morning when I drove along the Arno River as
far as the village of Montécchio, then turned right toward
Chiusi La Verna, the hill town at the foot of Mount Penna in
Tuscany. The mountain forests of the Casentino were already losing their leaves. Gold mingled with the deep green of conifers as
groves of chestnut trees finally abandoned their summer garb.
Winter was suddenly upon us, promising long evenings and fires
glowing in the grate, grappa poured in coffee to enliven those
days of inactivity that lay ahead.

It had snowed the previous night. Now the hills were white
and seamlessly textured, the trees on the hilltop looking like they
had been dusted with powder. Drawing closer to the monastery
of La Verna, I couldn't help feeling a sense of anticipation, a fore-
boding almost, as if I were approaching something altogether different than any architectural monument. La Verna was not simply
a mountain, a cliff-face, or a wilderness dedicated to the inwardness of nature; it was perhaps the most significant place in Italy,
indeed in all Europe. For here a man had sought to approach the
power of the Invisible and render it palpable for everyone.

I'm talking about Saint Francis of Assisi, the son of a middle-class linen merchant named Pietro di Bernardone. Much has been made of this man's gifts, his penitential genius, and his ability to inspire those who came in contact with him. What he stood for— the near-perfect imitation of Christ—has trickled down to us through the ages, a rivulet of aspiration and hope. Of all the Christian saints he more than most showed that it was possible to lead a simple life entirely dependent upon the good will of others. Money and possessions meant nothing to him. He gave away all that he owned in order to pursue a more difficult existence— that of refashioning himself into someone capable of experiencing a genuine surplus of being.

I don't want to go into all the details of his remarkable life as these are well documented. Let me just say that he was more than a simple pilgrim who liked to deliver sermons and homilies from the steps of town squares throughout Umbria. Of course there was a great deal of the orator about him; he rather enjoyed an audience. But he was no Savonarola preaching hellfire and eternal damnation to those who chose not to heed his message. Rather, he was a man who had witnessed some authentic and unquestionable event that set him apart. Francis had encountered a frisson, a shudder of excitement, so intense, so otherworldly, so outside the realm of normal human experience that he found it impossible to remain silent. Unlike the hermits of the Egyptian desert who preferred silence in the face of the Absolute, Francis was a man in league with words.

He had come to Montefeltro, in Romagna, with his companion Leo in the spring of 1213 on his way to Morocco, some say to preach to the unconverted. I suspect it was also to talk with the sages in Fez and Marrakech, if not those living in Moorish Spain. There's a tradition suggesting that Francis was deeply influenced not only by troubadour poetry, itself derived from Arab song and associated Sufic elements, but that when he journeyed to Egypt and Syria in the summer of 1219 to join the Crusade, and later met with Sultan Malik al-Kamil, it was not solely to argue the supremacy of Christian belief over that of Islam as the chroniclers so carefully relate. Rather, it was to explore with the sages of Egypt the subtle mysticism of their thought, and to learn thereby.[1]

At Montefeltro that spring day he was invited to a banquet in the nearby castle of Saint Leo, to celebrate the knighthood of one of the Counts of Montefeltro. Given his enthusiasm for public speaking, he couldn't help but make one of his speeches to the assembled populace. Up he climbed on a low wall, his protruding ears more animated than usual, and spoke with such fervor and grace that people forgot why they had come to the banquet. The gist of his sermon that day was this: "So great is the good which I expect, that all pain is to me a delight." A certain Orlando of Chiusi was on hand to hear him, and being so affected by the "wonderful things" he heard from the mouth of Francis, he called the man aside and made him an extraordinary offer.

"In Tuscany I possess a mountain that is most favorable to the things of the spirit," Count Orlando said. "It is very secluded and wild and well situated for one who seeks the solitary life. If it pleases you, I will gladly present it to you and your companions for the salvation of my soul." Thus Francis found himself the owner of a mountain. This man who denied the value of owning anything had suddenly become a landholder!

✻ ─────────

1. One chronicler wrote of the meetings between Francis and Malik al-Kamil at the time of the siege of Damietta by the Crusaders: "The Sultan not only dismissed Francis in peace, with wonder and admiration for the man's unusual qualities, but *received him fully into his favor* [our italics], gave him a safe-conduct by which he might go and come, with *full permission to preach to his sub-* *jects,* and an entreaty that he would frequently return to visit him." Certainly, this suggests that the sultan regarded Francis as more than a mere fellow traveler, nor did he appear to pose a threat to the orthodoxy of Islam. In fact, it rather suggests that Francis may have been sympathetic to many Muslim beliefs.

In the name of his fledgling order Francis agreed to accept La
Verna as a place of retreat. Of course he had no way of knowing
how important the spot would become for Christians throughout the world. Nor did he have any intimation of how prophetic
his sermon at Montefeltro might turn out to be. "So great is the
good which I expect, that all pain is my delight" may have been
little more than a pious cliché until the moment when he too
experienced the likeness of a Crucified Man on his body. All he
had done that day was gratefully accept the gift of a mountain in
the name of his youthful order of friars—a place that was to become a true mountain of visions.

My journey that snow-driven morning was made less with
the expectation of encountering such a vision. I was content with
the idea of being in its proximity only, so that I too might be
rendered capable of at least contemplating what others, at best,
had so far inadequately described. Is not the reason for making
such journeys the desire to participate, by some mysterious act
of immediacy, in an event that has been made timeless? I have
long held the belief that one can, if one is so inclined, begin to
reconstruct events in the imagination, and so extend their life
beyond what is considered their apparent time and place. Such
events are luminous. Like a dead star adrift in space they continue to radiate light long after their physical demise has passed.

Francis's stigmata is just such a star. I had been drawn to La
Verna because I believed this extraordinary event had indeed occurred—before dawn of the morning of September 14, 1224, to
be precise. To argue that it didn't happen, or that it might have
been little more than a "mystical event" is to denigrate observers
and historians alike. Others witnessed the event besides Francis.
Brother Leo said that at a distance he too "saw a seraph, a Burn-
ing One" when finally he recounted his memories shortly before
his death. Brother Leo's observations are further recorded: "He
looked up and gazed at the sky. And while he was looking, he saw

come down from the heights of Heaven a torch of flaming fire that was very beautiful and bright and pleasing to the eyes and that descended on Saint Francis's head. And he heard a voice come out of the flame and speak to Saint Francis." Certain farmers recalled that they awoke early and began to harness their pack animals, believing that dawn had already broken. It was only later, when the shimmering light of the seraph had died away, that they realized night was still upon them.[2]

So I knew I was traveling toward a place whose topography had been transfigured by some extraordinary event. The Stigmata, the taking upon oneself of the five wounds incurred by Christ at the time of his crucifixion, is more than an act of empathy with a dying Jesus. Clearly it has ramifications that extend beyond the events of the Passion and the suffering that it evokes. The cross, for all its heady symbolism, is still only a garrote, a legal instrument of execution. No—what the Crucifixion means, and by implication the Stigmata, is something far more unnerving than memories of a God-man becoming entangled in the legal system of Rome.

Arriving at the monastery at La Verna was therefore laden with significance for me. The ancient buildings, the courtyards, chapels and church, the rude grotto where the saint had slept, the

---

2. In a contemporary account known as *The Five Considerations on the Holy Stigmata*, the anonymous chronicler recounts: "All of Mount La Verna seemed to be on fire with very bright flames, which shone in the night and illumined the various surrounding mountains and valleys more clearly than if the sun were shining over the earth. The shepherds who were guarding their flocks in that area witnessed this. And they were gripped by an intense fear when they saw the mountain aflame and so much light around it, as they lately told the friars, declaring that the fiery light remained above Mount La Verna for an hour or more.... Likewise, because of the brightness of that light, which shone through the windows of the inns in the district, some muleteers who were going to Romagna got up, thinking that the sun had risen, and they saddled and loaded their animals. And while they were on their way, they saw the light cease and the real sun rise."

gift shop, hotel, and restaurant—these were all superfluous to the main event. They were physical accretions that inevitably gather about mysterious occurrences and so render them approachable, even harmless. I know from past experience that to journey to a place of power revered by the Aborigines of Australia, for example, is often unsettling. One is confronted by a profound sense of antiquity, of awe, sometimes even—yes—of terror. There's no getting away from it: ancient spiritual sites have a capacity to repel rather than to embrace. They preserve their luminosity by way of a scission, an abyss of separation: human beings are, and always will remain, apart from the Invisible.

In one respect, the monastery of La Verna, located as it is on the very spot where Francis received the Stigmata before dawn that morning, is little more than what one expects from a popular tourist destination. Its cherubic enameled terra-cotta reliefs by the Della Robbia family, the exaggerated posture depicted in statues of Saint Francis preaching to the birds in niches, the plastic flowers and electric candles that can be activated by little more than a small monetary offering—such pious images represent the comfortable side of religion. They offer a sanitized version of the mysterious, the awe-filled. The blood of the Stigmata, the pain of being stretched out and nailed to a cross, all that makes up the anguish and suffering of a humiliated God is somehow absent. Clearly La Verna today, and perhaps for the past hundreds of years, is no place for a many-winged seraph to re-appear in a blaze of light.

So why did I come? Why did I venture to a place whose meaning had all but been reduced to an image on a postcard? I suppose I needed to go back in my mind to what had happened there in the first place, in order to justify my journey. I needed to explore what it was about that mid-September cataclysm which not only frightened the local farmers and upset the stock, but sent shock waves throughout Christendom. After all, the transfer of

Christ's wounds to another person, the Stigmata, had never before occurred. But Francis's wounds were of a different order. What happened to Christ was a real event. The nails were manufactured in Palestine. The hammer, too, probably. People had witnessed this macabre ritual being played out while they stood around on Golgotha, perhaps making idle comments to those nearby. The Crucifixion was a public event. One could even argue that the criminals on both sides of Christ shared something of his martyrdom. The five wounds were less penitential than they were political, more a piece of stage management affirming the authority of Rome than a gesture to appease the Jews.

Christ had made claims that no man before him had done: that he was God. He had gone even further by saying that no man could come to the Father save through him. These were provocative remarks. They were dangerous, too. If a man could make these claims for himself, if he could assert his divinity even as he continued to live as an ordinary man of flesh and blood, then he was assuming for himself certain powers denied to everyone else. By setting himself up as a paragon, he had made it difficult for many to identify with him as a man. This perhaps was his dilemma—too much the God, he had failed to pay enough concern to his manhood.

But is it really true? Obviously Francis didn't believe so. He had dedicated his entire life to emulating Christ's quixotic and sometime peripatetic behavior. Living among lepers and the poor, rebuilding shrines, preaching, spurning property and dismissing his family from his life, practicing celibacy and subjecting himself to extreme acts of penitence (he wasn't averse to flagellation, we are told), wandering the country like a footloose tramp, clearly Francis was not your average man about town. Nor was medieval society, as bourgeois as it had become, used to the idea of seeing a man standing in the town square stark naked, while dismissing his parents from his life in the process! It wasn't prepared either to understand someone who denied every value that it held dear. Property, money, possessions, a stable place of residence, family ties, citizenship as a cherished ideal—these were anathema to Francis. He simply refused to allow the unbounded impotence of his contemporaries to rob him of the life that he wanted. What he saw lacking in his fellow citizens was a belief in the free course of the world as a place without envy.

I suspect this is what made him so different, so ready to fulfill some unusual task. I say "task" because it occurs to me that Francis was aware of his destiny more than most. Whatever he'd experienced early in his life, whatever he'd confronted within himself had obviously inspired him to a course of action that none had embarked upon before. He'd made his entire being into a lightning rod capable of attracting the most powerful of energies— that of discovering, for the first time, what Nietzsche called the "man in man." This new type of man he was looking for in himself had none of the hallmarks of the old. He wanted to become someone who possessed the courage to prize open the door to the holy so that the divine might enter and claim him entirely.

A strange predicament to find oneself in. Yet it probably lay at the back of my thoughts prior to entering La Verna that morning. The snow on the ground masked the cobbles, so that their starkness was made more acute by the footprints of an earlier visitor. The forest on either side was glazed in icicles, each one a filament of sunlight. Strange, contorted rock shapes loomed, suggesting some seismic upheaval. Could the mountain have retained vestiges of those powerful forces unleashed nearly eight hundred years ago? Had there been some interchange between a man and a mountain? Were the wounds of the Stigmata still lying like humus in the ground, awaiting some new act of gestation? I asked myself these questions as I approached the various sites associated with Francis.

His bed, for example, lay at the end of a dark chasm. Here on a cold piece of rock he had spent the Lent of Saint Michael, the time from the feast of the Assumption to the feast of Saint Michael the Archangel. He had crossed over to this rocky spot by way of a log bridge placed there by friends. He had decided to isolate himself completely during this period of meditation and prayer. "Go back to your place and leave me alone," he entreated the friars. "I intend spending this Lent here without distraction or disturbance of mind. None of you must come to me. Brother Leo, come only once a day with a little bread and water. At the hour of matins come silently, and when you reach the end of the log, just say: '*Domine, labia mea aperies.*' If I answer, '*Et os meum annuntiabit laudem tuam,*' come across to my cell, so that we might say matins together. But if I do not reply at once, go right back."[3]

Here indeed was a man who'd set himself an impossible task: to renovate Christianity through a supreme act of abnegation. He wanted to utterly destroy himself, and so bring to others the prospect of uncovering the true person in themselves. During those days in retreat Francis managed to will himself into a condition where he could hear, as if by way of some supra-auditory perception, the very cogitations of the stone about him. He had entered what can best be described as a "primordial cloud" whereby he was ready, and prepared, for the moment when the Divine might finally reveal itself. Francis had so lost his senses that he was able to experience the Divine Sigh as a breath of light pouring down upon him.

I knew that I was treading on thin ice. Even as I entered the chapel of the Blessed Stigmata, I sensed that I was skirting one of the truly significant events in the history of Christianity. No one,

---

3. Francis's loss of sense is confirmed by contemporary chroniclers: "Sometimes he was so rapt in God that he could not talk for a night and a day, and he did not hear or feel anything with his bodily senses. Yet Brother Leo very carefully observed the saint's order."

not in the least Francis, has ever been able to suitably convey the awesome nature of what happened to him on that September morning. How could they? How could he? Words offer a paltry palette when it comes to trying to paint the events of that night. Many have tried, and as many have been reduced to a simple explanation: Francis received the wounds of the divine ineffability and so re-enacted the suffering of the death of Christ. Lance and nails invaded his body to the point where his whole being took upon itself the pain of the Crucifixion. He had, so to speak, mystically died as a co-sufferer with the Son of God. In his biography of the saint, *Legendae maior et minor*, Saint Bonaventure wrote:

ON A CERTAIN MORNING, about the feast of the Exaltation of the Cross, while he was praying on the mountainside, he saw a seraph with six wings, fiery and shining, descend from the sublimity of heaven. And when the seraph's swift flight had brought him near to the man of God, there appeared between his wings the form of a man crucified, with his hands and feet extended in the fashion of a cross, and fixed to the cross....The saint was overcome with a great wonder at this sight, and joy mingled with pain filled his heart....

The vision then vanished, leaving in the heart of the saint a wonderful fervor, and a no less wonderful imprint of the marks in his flesh. In his hands and his feet forthwith began to appear the marks of the nails, just as he had seen them but a little before in the form of the Crucified One. His hands and feet seemed to have been pierced through the center by the nails, the heads of which were in the palms of the hands and the upper part of the feet, and the points behind. And the heads of the nails were round and black, with the points, oblong and sharp, twisted and almost bent back, so that, transfixing the flesh, they protruded from it. The flesh of the right side also, as if pierced by a lance, was broken by a red wound, from which flowed the sacred blood, staining the habit about his thighs.

✳

There is a medieval concreteness about these remarks. They speak of the fascination people in that time felt about exact observation. No one can say this is a vague account, or that it fails to convey how a stigmata is received. There is no fudging here. What happened to Francis is evident enough, too: he was visited by a seraph and metaphorically crucified. But more importantly, he *spoke* to God. He asked Him three questions, questions that go to the very heart of all our inquiries about otherness and the origin of being. They were: "Who are You, my dearest God?" "What am I?" and "Why do you visit me?" They are reminiscent of the questions Paul Gauguin asked himself in one of his greatest paintings completed several hundred years later, on the island of Tahiti: "Who am I? Where am I going? What am I doing here?" They are the fundamental questions of existence.

At this point God made a strange demand of Francis. He asked him to put his hand inside the folds of his habit near his breast and bring forth whatever he found there. "I searched and found a gold coin that was so large and bright and beautiful, like one I had never seen before in the world. This I offered to God," Francis relates.

God said to Francis again: "Make me another offering as before."

To which Francis replied: "I don't have, nor do I love, nor do I want anything but You. Gold I despise. If there's anything more to be found in my breast, You alone put it there. So I return it to You."

Francis made the offer of a gold coin to God three times. It was only after the third offering that he realized the significance of the gifts: they were the gold of obedience, of poverty, and the golden radiance of chastity. These were God's gift to him. As soon as he understood the nature of the exchange, Francis immediately felt something come over him. He had, as he said, felt his soul "so infused with God that my entire being became an act of praise for His Person." In these dramatic moments Francis made himself into an instrument of the Divine, a vessel for the spirit of God.

We are left with the symbols only. A seraph, a Crucified Man nestled in its wings, and three gold coins, the currency of God. Each in its own way says a great deal about the unusual work habits of divinity. It deals in images, of course, knowing that only in images is the mind capable of being vitalized by the will. If we take the trouble to strip such images of their palpable nature, however, all we're left with are a seraphic apparition, the instruments of execution, and a principle of monetary exchange. Viewed in this way they mean very little; but evoked as images they have the power to transform a man forever. As the ancient chronicles relate, Francis didn't so much endure a physical martyrdom when he received the likeness of the Christ Crucified; rather, an "enkindling of the mind" enlivened him. The Stigmata was just this: a self-overflowing, an infusion of a superabundance of life that can only come when a man has finally turned away from himself.

Where did all this leave me? Unfortunately, in the chapel of the Blessed Stigmata, I didn't feel that my mind had been very much enkindled. The Della Robbia crucifixion above the altar was too elegant, too refined to press home any claims to spiritual enrichment on my behalf. Nor had the artist succeeded in capturing the enormity of the event that had occurred under the marble tiles beneath my feet. Somewhere below the level of the floor lay a stone on the edge of a chasm where Francis had knelt to receive the Stigmata. A stone inscribed in Latin marked the spot, and was visible through glass inlaid in the floor. But I sensed that it was a concession to reality only, that no one really knew where he had knelt.

It was only when I had retreated from the chapel of the Blessed Stigmata, and noticed a set of steps leading down into the ancient oratory of Saint Bonaventure, that something began to happen for me. I could feel it. The oratory was simpler in construction, being no more than a low room carved out of the very rock on which Francis had knelt. In a niche above the altar his effigy stood. Plastic flowers in vases were arranged on either side. A small window to the left looked out onto the valley below. Light streamed through the opening, making the use of candles redundant. By accident I found myself all but carved into that moment when Francis had received a visitation from the seraph. Now I knew I was in the proximity of one of the most poignant events in the history of human consciousness.

"These are the emblems of my Passion," Christ announced, out of the wings of the seraph. "May you be my standard-bearer."

I could hear his words. I could see the feathered wings of the seraph bathed in unbearable whiteness. I could feel the perturbations of the spirit as it descended into words. It's no easy task for a disembodied being to master the idiosyncrasies of language, since it is more at home dealing in images. But this one had. It had alerted me to the sufferings of Christ Crucified, and how such an event had occurred. I suddenly realized that it is we who are responsible for the death of God. And it is we who have set about destroying the divine in ourselves.

Francis's stigmata reminded me of the singular power of penetration: how cross and nail are but instruments of dalliance with the most dangerous weapon of all, that of hubris. When we kill the divine in ourselves we embark on a life of self-destruction and so become creatures of nihilation, of nothingness. If the Stigmata has anything to say to us today, then it must be to alert us to the risks that we run in our bid to control nature. The Stigmata is a link between ourselves and the forces of chaos that unwittingly support us. If we try to master these forces in a way that benefits humankind only, to the detriment of matter itself, then we run the risk of killing off the divine for good. I began to realize that this was the message of the seraph, that six-winged creature whose home is in a cloud of unknowing that we so rarely deign to visit.

In Saint Bonaventure's chapel, deep in the rock, I had crossed a chasm. For the first time I had journeyed beyond myself into the inestimable reaches of the other. Though I was no beneficiary of the Stigmata, at least I understood it better. Francis had been wounded by his time. As a way of healing that wound he'd been granted the opportunity to receive the ultimate gift, that of the wounds of the dying Christ. Deity's suffering pulsated through his entire body. Deity's encounter with humankind's destructive impulse was imprinted on his limbs. Deity's retreat from this world in the wake of betrayal, false accusation, and judicial condemnation remained on his body, emblems of the supreme sacrifice.

I kept thinking, too, of what might be the final effect of the Stigmata on Francis. Though he carried these wounds on his body for the rest of his days, daily needing to bathe and dress them, he always recognized that their symbolism went beyond the act of suffering itself. For him, surely, the "enkindling of the mind" was what they truly embodied: a mind transformed into a living torch capable of lighting the way beyond mere semblance, appearance, or correctness—a mind able to chart a course through the shoals of knowledge as power, of knowledge as a reliquary of man's self-assertiveness: such was the kind of mind Francis might have struggled to realize all his life.

The idea of the mind as fire was a suitable image to take away from the monastery of La Verna. This image said a great deal. It told me that such a gift more than compensated for any loss I might have suffered through my own waywardness, or my own

compromise with the invisible gestures of the spirit on those occasions when they'd beckoned. I was reminded of one of Francis's
miracles where he cured a child suffering from a cruel ulcer. He
made the Sign of the Cross over the wound three times, and the
boy was healed. The next morning, when the child's mother went
to comfort him, she found the bandage had disappeared. Where
the ulcer had once been, the flesh had grown over in the form of
a red rose.

This mental fire bestowed on Francis had also been bestowed
on me—not, I now realized, as the Stigmata but as a rose. The red
rose of intellect, of the courage to think beyond the evident, beyond the merely comprehensible, the plausible—surely this is what
Francis had experienced, too. Alone among the men of his time
he'd been devoured by a thirst for immediacy, to destroy all the
evidence of his previous life, and to build a new world within
himself whatever the cost. In doing so, Francis had revealed the
mysterious nature of his path—to journey beyond the white wings
of the seraph, to accept the wounds of inefficacy and impotence,
and finally to fashion what was left into the miracle of a red rose.

I'd traveled to La Verna on the first day of winter to be greeted
by my own revelation. That wintered landscape of old chapels,
grottos, frescoes, relics, and snow-clad trees still hungered after a
new encounter with the seraph. I could feel it. Though Francis
had long since departed on his journey into the metropolis of
minds the world over, he had nonetheless left his trace on this
mountain in Tuscany. All his actions were those of a madman
who sought sanity outside the preserve of good sense. I liked him
for that. He was a man after my own heart. I began to think that
I shared with him at least an anticipation, if not a visitation by
the seraph. For me the Stigmata was no longer a sign of anguish.
It had been transformed into a bloom of inordinate grace.

CHAPTER TWO

If Stones
Could Speak

✳

I've said that Francis was in league with words, that silence
was not his forte. Let me amend this. He enjoyed silence as
much as language. Few before him had dabbled so successfully, and with so much effect, in disputation, dialectic, even rheto-
ric—aside from his clear need to seek out solitude at different
times during his life. This paradox made him a confusing character even for those of his own time. People were not used to
meeting in one man a theologian, a poet, a politician, and an
anchorite. It made them suspect that he might be mad, or at least
partly imbued with malign spirits. Francis was already on the road
to becoming a post-medieval, for he had discovered that utterance could be successfully honed in silence. Words could be in-
ternalized there, and so re-fashioned to carry a greater burden of
subjectivity.

Francis loved to withdraw to remote spots in the Tuscan and
Umbrian countryside. There was a long tradition of anchorites
in Europe, so it was not considered unusual for a monk to withdraw from society and seek out the company of nature. The tradition went as far back as the Egyptian anchorites of the Nitria

Desert and the lonely caves of Saint Anthony and Saint Paul, high up in the mountains flanking the Red Sea. There the early Christians did battle with the devil, lived on bread and water, while slowly deepening their consciousness to the point where it was transformed into a well of simplicity and wisdom. This was the payoff for living a life of solitude: the hermit took refuge in the desert in order to live outside history, and so learned how to converse with angels.

I managed to visit a number of places where Francis chose to retreat from the world as I made my away about Central Italy. In Lake Trasimeno, on the island of Maggiore, I discovered a cave where he spent Lent one year. At Le Celle, outside the walls of Cortona, lies a monastery dedicated to a cave that he had dug for himself in 1211. And also at a place known as San Illuminato near Alviano in southern Umbria, I discovered a crypt where he'd spent a long period in solitude. Nearby there are ruins of a tiny hermitage founded by the Camaldolites in 1006. The broken arches and discarded columns of the medieval chapel lie on the ground, a testament to what must have been a poignant and dreamy spirituality that survived for centuries in these hills.

Walking about the nave and choir of this ruined chapel, among the white stones lying in the grass, I felt a powerful sense of words sung, of a breviary uttered, of a prayer whispered into the silence of the place. It has been said that the muteness of nature retains a sense of sadness, and that all nature would begin to lament if it were endowed with language. Speechlessness becomes the great sorrow of nature. If the stones of San Illuminato could speak, I suspect they would agree with this observation. Nature's disinclination to communicate, perhaps because it is always in a state of mourning, is a language of its own—the language of the unknowable. To name a thing is to enter into the deepest linguistic reason for melancholy, once a thing is known.

Did Francis intuit this? A part of his charm is that he seemed able to enter into converse with nature. He was a sort of wild man, a primitive, who was capable of making his own silence into the rudiments of dialogue. Much of what he said is less profound than it is self-evident. If that were his only contribution to the human adventure, then perhaps he might have gone unnoticed. There's no doubt that he did enjoy talking with animals and birds, and that they enjoyed speaking with him, too. We are therefore alerted to some other energy at work in the man. He was trying to discover a way of expression that transcended the limitation of words.

The grottos he retreated to in order to pray and meditate are a kind of early laboratory of the spirit. The one at San Illuminato for example was graced with a stone lintel on which had been carved the word "Crypta." But, strangely—or was it a gesture on the part of nature?—a layer of vine had fallen over the word, partly obscuring it. What I initially read was the word "Cry." At once I recognized that nature was speaking to me, not with its own words but with mine. I was gazing upon the tears of Francis as he struggled to reconcile himself to the impossibility of bridging the gap between himself and divinity.

This event struck me as important. The narrow cave in which Francis once slept reminded me of a prehistoric shelter I had visited in the Sahara Desert. I think I imagined Francis as a latter-day Paleolithic person, content to while away his time under the cooling influence of stone. Its very inertness suggested to me something that the rest of us wouldn't even dream of—that is, the prospect of attaining to a state of rapture through converse with earth.

Now the old meaning of the word *rapture* was "abduction," a forcible carrying-off. In Francis's day the word would have still possessed these connotations. The forcible movement of someone from one place to another suggested by *rapture* also implies a transportment, a bodily going-out of one's senses. It was said of Francis by a friend after one of these bouts in a cave that he emerged a different man than the one who had gone in: "His countenance shone, dazzling to the beholder, and it seemed as though Francis was no longer the same man I had lately beheld entering the cavern." He had, in a sense, been carried off to another place, a place of rapture.

These caves and grottos scattered throughout Umbria and Tuscany are not unlike prehistoric ritual sites. But instead of taking off his clothing in their vicinity and dancing about a fire, or daubing the walls with exotic images of cult figures, Francis chose a more subtle path. He journeyed into himself. He had a penchant for interior dialogue. Of course he gave it the name "prayer" and talked of listening to the words of God. He may have phrased it in this way, I suspect, to allay the fears of those less educated who stood beside him. This is the language they were used to hearing, as it was the language of pious exchange. But it seems to me that Francis had more problematic issues to deal with. He was trying to discover a way of bridging that gap I spoke of earlier, the gap between humankind and the Invisible.

It has been said that the idea of truth did not come into the world naked but rather as an image. This idea suggests that language has nothing to do with the revelation of truth. Much later, another lonely man, Frederich Nietzsche, observed that we possess art in order not to perish from the truth. Essentially they say the same thing: that the Invisible expresses itself only through the power of the image. Art is the one method by which we can denounce the stabilization of sheer appearance, the externality of the object in relation to how we see it, of which truth is its manifest illusion. Only through art are we able to wonder about ourselves.

I believe this to be the essence of what Francis was trying to do. The problem of truth for him was not one that could be explained by theology. He was well aware that such a system of thought was there to stabilize truth in a form that could be regarded as acceptable, but at the same time as illusory. The Church was the guardian of such theological systems, and espoused them quite naturally. There was nothing wrong in that. But when it came to wanting to devise a new language, a new way of approaching the inexpressible, it was no use going back to those old methods of stabilization. All that did was ossify existing thought. Francis, I'm quite sure, had no intention of allowing his vivid imagination, or his curiosity, to be contained by the heavy hand of dogma.

So he attempted to devise a new method of overcoming the problem. He took to the hills, literally. He decided that what he had to do was in the nature of a renovation. He needed to subject his mind and body to a series of tests, not so much to break his will—or, as he said, to drive Brother Donkey to the point of mental and physical exhaustion—but to see whether it was possible to extract some new insight out of all this self-punishment. His body, and his mind, became an anvil upon which he attempted to hammer out certain values, ones that would challenge human beings to create goals above themselves and their history.

It was no easy task. Francis was fully aware of the difficulties. The medieval Church, in part, had grown sclerotic. It spent a good deal of its time attempting to root out heresy wherever it arose, or conducting ill-conceived crusades to the Holy Land, or excommunicating emperors and kings for failing to support the papacy, while at the same time indulging in simony and nepotism. A large organization, owning vast estates throughout Europe, the Church wielded a power that only emperors could match. No one dared to confront it except in military terms. Any voice of dissent was crushed either by sword or Inquisitorial fire. For Francis to propose a new language of the spirit during these times demanded an entirely different approach. He would have to exercise authority by invoking a powerful moral force from within the Church itself.

Francis had to devise a new way of being. More importantly, he would have to do so by engaging in a life of subversion. On the one hand, he would insist on the rights and privileges of the papacy in matters of doctrinal orthodoxy and belief; while on the other he would make a case, by his own actions, to a life that denied the importance of hierarchy and spiritual privilege altogether. He would all but undermine the medieval Church by proposing a new ideal, an ideal based upon the teaching and practice of Christ.

Of course this idea wasn't new. What was new was that Francis saw it as a point of departure, not as an end in itself. He argued that poverty, chastity, and obedience were not simply the accouterments of a religious, but the basis for a heroic way of life. By genuinely living these and making them the leitmotif of existence, it was possible to embark upon a new kind of crusade, a crusade of the spirit. Is there any wonder that on a number of occasions he dreamed of going off on a crusade to the Holy Land? At one stage he even set out for the south of Italy, to Apulia, to join Walter of Brienne against the Normans.[1] Little did he know that the crusade he had embarked upon was not in keeping with his instincts.

According to Thomas of Celano, his first biographer, Francis was visited by a strange dream at that time: "Because Francis was eager for glory, he [that is, God] enticed him and raised his spirits with a vision of the heights of glory. For it seemed to Francis that his whole home was filled with the trappings of war, namely

---

1. This event occurred before Francis had adopted the habit. He had hoped to join Walter of Brienne, the leader of the papal forces of Innocent III in south- ern Italy. The pope had dubbed the expedition a "crusade" in the hope of generating a larger contingent of men, of which Francis was one.

saddles, shields, lances, and other things....He wondered silently within him what this could mean....The answer was conveyed to him that all these arms would be given to his soldiers. When he awoke, he arose in the morning with a glad heart, and considered the vision an omen of great success. He felt sure that his journey to Apulia would come out well."

Of course it didn't. Rather, he had misinterpreted the dream. This call to arms wasn't an invitation to enter the safe haven of the soldier, the life of bravado and military activity that he'd assumed was his. Francis had been deceived by his own fantasies into believing that his destiny lay in doing battle with the anti-papal forces of the south, when in reality the imagery of the dream invited him to do battle with an altogether different adversary, namely himself. The language of the Invisible, which at this stage in his career he had not yet encountered, remained impenetrable. The youthful zealot headed south armed to the teeth (and with the material support of his father), only to find himself waylaid in Spoleto by another dream while lying in bed feeling decidedly ill.

Saint Bonaventure, another of his biographers, suggests that in this second dream his dialogue with God took on a more direct tone: "Who can do more for you, Francis? The rich man or the poor?" Francis replied that clearly the rich man advantaged him more. "Then why seek out the servant rather than the master?" Francis was nonplused by this remark, and asked what he might do. "Return home. Wait there for the call. When it comes, act."

Thomas of Celano made an interesting observation on the Apulia fiasco. After the visitation by God, Francis "was so filled with joy that he could not contain himself, and, though he did not want to, he uttered some strange things to the ears of men. Though he could not keep silent, he nonetheless spoke cautiously, and *in an obscure manner* [Thomas's italics]. He spoke to his special friend of a hidden treasure. But to others he only spoke figuratively." At once we begin to see Francis struggling to express what had happened. Language was beginning to fail him. He was coming up against barriers that prohibited him from saying outright what had occurred. In the end he resorted to a new technique of expression when he finally confessed: "I shall take a more noble and more beautiful spouse than you have ever seen," in reply to someone who asked him whether he intended getting married. But no one inquired as to what kind of marriage he really had in mind.

All this is the talk of a man who possessed a secret. From this point on Francis knew that he had to be very careful about what he said. It may be that his frequent wanderings throughout Italy, Spain, France, and Outremer or the Holy Land, were a part of an attempt to escape the consequences of the prosaic. By absenting himself for long periods from the affairs of the order that he had helped to set up, all he managed to do was mystify his presence. Whatever he said or did became an object of portent, and became in itself its own metaphor. He, Francis, had learned how to journey beyond himself in the act of embracing the road.

There's no doubt that he was aware of his power over others. So acute was his self-consciousness that he measured all others along side of it. He magnified his personal faults to the point where they seemed to be overwhelming. Whereas, for others, such faults might be regarded as no more than character flaws, Francis saw his own as deeply disruptive to the process of renovation that he was engaged in. There was nothing psychological about Francis, thankfully; otherwise his actions would have fallen into the category of one psychosis or another. Freud had not yet come along to dig into his problematical relationship with his father or the silent, loving acceptance of his mother. If he had, then he would have likely come across the image of the absent father (Pietro di Bernardone spent a good deal of his time in France buying cloth), a child at home in the loving arms of his mother, Pica (herself French and so, in a sense, of exotic stock), and a son who had been disinherited of his name Giovanni (his mother's full name was Giovanna) in favor of Francis by his father. France, the absent land of his father's dreams, was bestowed on him as a name after his birth on his father's return to Assisi, almost as if Pietro wished to deny his son's origins and his wife's wish to call him John. The child had become, in a sense, transformed into a "foreign land" and deprived of the bosom. Moreover he had become representative of an exclusion—his father's.

One has to go back and study the behavior of Pietro. Most biographers see him as unsympathetic to his son's later ambitions, a tyrant who tried to force Francis into the family business. It may be true. But I see Pietro as a man afflicted by his time. He was a member of the urban merchant class, and so despised—and was despised—by the aristocrats who lived outside the walls of Assisi in their castles. Such men did little to augment the wealth of the community, except to levy taxes, exact tolls, and bleed the peasants. As a self-made man, Pietro was opposed to the aura of privilege that clung to their class. Pietro's merchant status may have encouraged him to want to see a new order established in Assisi, one founded upon the principle of hard work, enterprise, and industry.

Clearly all the evidence suggests that he saw the world in material terms. At the same time, he may have been exposed to a branch of Cathar dualism encountered in Provencal France, or even in the northern Italian towns that he passed through. His conversation at home after his buying trips could easily have been filled with talk of good and evil as individual entities, and of the spiritual rigor of the Cathar priests in their bid to balance these opposing forces. Pietro may have found some affinity with the Cathars because their religion did not represent an entrenched dogma, nor did it espouse the principle of hierarchy as clearly as did that of the Church. Pietro may have felt he was among like-minded people when he tramped the back roads between Foix and Carcassonne, Albi and Beziers. The Cathars were free spirits in a world of institutionalized privilege, both secular and sacred. Their language was the language of a new kind of freedom—that of a people standing up for their own comprehension of divinity, and the right to take charge of their own lives as a result.

It was vestiges of this kind of spiritual anarchy that Pietro di Bernardone may have tried to instill into his son. Francis was to be the bearer of all that was best from France. An unorthodox approach to religion, a distant language, and a troubadour poetry that attempted to give expression to those fledgling aspirations of a people who were intellectually and spiritually on the move—these were what Pietro wanted his son to imbibe. Cathar France represented the unraveling of medieval Europe; what the movement wished to replace it with did not occur until much later, however, during the fourteenth and fifteenth centuries, with the birth of the individual as someone superior to either state or Church. In the twelfth and thirteenth centuries, guild affiliations rather than character still defined a man's identity.

In the meantime, Francis was brought up an alien in his own town. Exposed to Cathar ideas of dualism from an early age, at least in terms of the idea of bodily self-sacrifice and discipline, a singer of troubadour songs, the son of a largely absent father, he was left to his own devices. I suspect his very freedom as the son of a well-to-do merchant only heightened his disillusionment with the way things were done in medieval Assisi. They say he was a gay blade, the boy about town, but this fact was only part of the concealment he practiced in order to veil his real conflict. Francis had already decided on his course of action long before the dreams and portents of his biographers pointed the way. He had come to the conclusion that only in a deliberate act of rejection could he hope to become the man he wanted to be.

That meant to distance himself from all authority, be it civic, familial, or spiritual. In this way he chose a path that went far beyond any dreamed up in France or northern Italy. The Cathar leaders, for example, expected men and women to submit to the ultimate rejection of procreation as a means of resisting evil. The troubadours, for all their gaiety and non-conventional mode of comportment, were still in league with *fin' amor*, a distant love, as a means of defying the regime of marriage, which they saw as a mere contract. Both the Cathars and the troubadours were, in their different ways, committed to the idea of barrenness, to a lack of fecundity as an ideal in human relations. Reproduction became anathema to a people who saw their fertility as little more than liegeman to the old aristocratic temper.

I know it might sound strange that sexuality—or the lack of it—was central to Francis's perception of the birth of any new, spiritualized being. Some may even argue that his denial of the body was an aberration, that all it did was contribute to a general sense of self-loathing that pervades Christianity anyway. Physical denial has its opponents. It is seen as a turning away from sensate reality in favor of what is, at most, an attenuated vision of the inner person. The desexualized being becomes someone who undermines the primacy of the sensual as a way of attaining control over men's minds. The monk, the nun, and the priest are *per se* those who invest their bodies with an aura of sanctity through this act of denial. For other, harsher judges, such an act is no more than a collective deceit on the part of the Church.

Of course Francis suffered from this collective deceit too. He was a man of his time. We cannot get away from the fact that he regarded women with a good deal of suspicion (not dislike, let me emphasize). At the same time he exhorted his followers to look upon their bodies as Brother Donkey, a beast of burden, good for carrying about its sack of flesh and bones and nothing more. The mind and, more importantly, its *intentions* had to be borne by some physical dimension, but let no one celebrate the physical at the expense of the thoughtful process of detachment that asceticism was meant to inspire. We are a far cry here from the athletes at Olympia competing nude for the prize of a wreath being placed on their heads.

Sexual abstinence was a deeply ingrained principle of denial. For the Cathars it was a form of narcissism, since it encouraged the idea that a true man, a true spiritual being, should always live in a state of awareness about his terminal state. His own cessation, lived fully and with dedication, was the only way of combating evil, since evil demanded its pound of flesh in the form of continuance, in the very act of procreation itself. To deny evil its deep need to gorge upon a man's desire for immortality was to starve evil into submission. The voluntary destruction of the body, its appetites and desires, was a participation in an act of severance: the soul was finally separated from matter. To love God was to love the possibility of dying.

I suspect that underneath it all Francis concurred with this idea. Of course, he would never have articulated it, but he lived it nonetheless. He regarded his body as a palimpsest upon which a new divinity might be inscribed. This divinity was linked to his desire to imitate what he believed was Christ's exhortation: "Love your enemies and do good to those who hate you" (Mt 5:44). By an extraordinary leap of logic Francis managed to interpret this to mean: "Let us hate our bodies with its vices and its sins....Living according to the flesh the devil wishes to deprive us of eternal life, and so cast us into hell." Once more the body has been denied its role as a temple of the spirit.[2]

---

2. These remarks are taken from the first Rule devised by Francis in 1221 for his order. Much of it was incorporated in the Rule that received papal sanction in 1223.

When I looked about me at the ruins of San Illuminato, I was troubled. The nave and capitals had fallen in disarray. Arch and apse lay about like prehistoric bones. In a cow stall nearby the smell of chaff reminded me that stock had long since made these ruins their home rather than monks. By the crypt of Saint Francis stood a tiny effigy of the saint on a rock, with flowers, coins, and a plastic wolf at its feet. So simple was its effect that it reminded me of a lingam in a Hindu temple. There was no blood splashed against the rock, but I did sense that some form of offering had been made. I began to think that surely pilgrims to this place must divine the sublime eroticism of Francis, in spite of his body-denial. In effigy he had become insensate, a primeval stone, the offering of all those who see Christ's celibacy as a kind of ecstatic orgasm of the soul.

It made me wonder whether it might be more than language that was the reef upon which Francis had finally grounded himself. Of course he used words with the same canny zeal as any proselyte. Of course every biblical text he could lay his hands on became a part of his armory if it could be found to support his argument. Of course he possessed a talent for inverting thought to his own advantage.[3] No one denies that. What I continued to find fascinating about his personality, however, was his ability to bring the complexity of belief into such sharp focus. His intelligence, wedded as it was to the wildness of the Umbrian countryside and his own need to be a part of it, had learned how to discern

※ ─────────────

3. A good example is the following. When asked why God had chosen him over another, he replied: "You want to know why me? Why? Because God did not find a greater sinner than me, or one more simple and foolish. So he chose me because he has chosen the foolish things of the world to put shame to the wise, and the base things of the world to bring to naught the noble and great and strong." Far from reflecting an illiterate or foolish person, Francis's remarks show him to be an extremely sophisticated thinker. His remarks are those of a dialectician rather than a simpleton.

things in the human psyche that otherwise might have gone unnoticed. Rather than words he used a sort of intensity, a
deep-down chrism of resolve to anoint people with the power
and rightness of his purpose. No one was a match for him, not
even popes.

The only person not to succumb to this extraordinary transformation of human nature was Francis's father, Pietro
Bernardone. His son had for some reason rejected the man who
had gone off to France in search of wealth and the heady polem-
ics of a competing belief. Between them we observe no intimation of either love or reconciliation. What happened? What had
so come between them that neither son nor father ever spoke to
one another again, so far as we know? Where does Pica's broken
heart fit into the family rift? Did anyone attempt to broker a peace
between an old cloth-merchant, down on his emotional luck, and
his religious reformer of a son whose very name had been
wrenched from him at birth?

These were the questions that arose in my mind as I wandered among the ruins of San Illuminato that day. Strangely, I
could feel the saint's presence. He was near me, perhaps lying on
the cold floor of his grotto, in a state of rapture at the sheer enormity of his task. The word "cry" on the lintel taunted me with its
tears. I knew then that Francis had been a man in greater conflict
with his circumstance than we will perhaps ever realize. What
lay ahead for him was not only the possibility of being loved
and reconciled to the Father—but also, belatedly, to Pietro
Bernardone.

CHAPTER THREE

The Naked Warrior

✳

S ometimes following in Francis's footsteps can turn out to
be an act of divergence. All the facts point to a certain path
that should be followed, but still one feels the need to wander off on byways. Medieval gyrovagues understood this well: they
spent their life tramping the back roads of Europe in a bid to
imprint space upon their brow. Unlike the monk in his monastery, the gyrovague spurned the fixity and discipline of living in
one place. He wanted something more—a sense that the world is
its own monastery, its own temple, its own tripod filled with the
flame of distance consuming every mile he traveled.

Sometimes I think of myself as a gyrovague, for I know that
Francis would have approved. He regarded the open road as his
primary place of residence, in spite of having been born into a
good home in Assisi. I suspect that his father's example as an
international cloth-merchant ensured that he would never remain in one place for too long. Why not go to Spain or Egypt if a
voice calls? The chivalry of the open road offers a rare freedom:
the chance to step beyond the walls that enclose oneself, and walk
into the broadness of the unknown.

On a forest path northwest of Assisi I came upon a small chapel built on the edge of a gorge. Its entrance faced the cliff beyond, and a distant waterfall. Initially I heard the cascade only, before noticing the slender thread of water plummeting into the gorge below. Yet when I stood at the entrance to the chapel and peered into its shadowy interior, I knew that I had discovered one of those rare objects of expansiveness that must have seduced Francis as easily as myself.

Inside, on the apse wall above the altar, was a fresco of the Virgin. In her slender fingers she held what looked like a piece of fruit, or a heart—it was hard to tell which. Painted in the Umbrian style, her beautiful face was lowered toward the Christ child who sat in her lap. On either side of the Madonna angels attended, their delicately painted wings a prism of color. The Virgin's expression was filled with a deep wonder at the sight of her child. But it was more than a mother-look that she conveyed; rather, I felt that I was in the presence of someone in a state of entrancement. Inwardness framed her eyes, her cheeks, and her lips. Holding her heart out toward the child, the Madonna delle Ripe had made her decision: the Christ child was worthy of this gift.

Such a place of tranquillity in the forest! Was it any wonder that Francis so much enjoyed the road? As old as Italy is, as steeped in history as its every stone appears to be, I couldn't help observing how a wintered landscape can still retain such strong links to what is an ancient heritage. The idea that a Jewish woman who had given birth to a child in faraway Palestine might end up on the wall of a chapel in Umbria struck me as a miracle in itself. She, the Mother of God, had managed to elbow aside all the many cult figures of the past, and put down roots of her own. She had brought with her from the East a certain purity, too, a generosity, and a love that surpassed all others. It was these qualities that transfigured the gorge outside the chapel, and made it bow before the spectacle of her gaze.

No one could argue that I wasn't treading a track through the forest that had been contemplated by wayfarers for countless centuries. Nor that, in Madonna delle Ripe, I hadn't come upon a manifestation of what was once known as the "soul of the path." It's a natural desire to want to invest nature with a deportment that is both visionary and sublime. This is why sanctuaries and chapels are built in certain places and not in others. There's something about one spot that sets it apart from another. I haven't been able to decide why this is so, except to say that such places actually feel different.

Francis had likely made his way along this track after experiencing one of the most traumatic events of his life. In his mid-twenties, he had suddenly made a decision that would change everything. A week or so before he had quit Assisi under conditions that would set him apart from his family, his friends, and to a certain extent his city. He would, in quite definite a manner, make a public gesture of abandoning the world. Moreover, he would finally denounce all allegiance to his father.

It was in 1207 that the event occurred. By this time Francis had gained a reputation as an eccentric, someone who may even have been a little mad. He'd attempted to rebuild a broken-down church outside the walls of Assisi by selling off some of his father's goods in Foligno, and making the money available to the reluctant priest for repairs. His obsession with rebuilding a chapel smacks of a man attempting to repair what was crumbling within himself. San Damiano was only the outward sign of Francis's conflict: its ruined walls spoke to him of despair and the collapse of his own fragmentary self. Francis, at this stage, was a man in search of a new persona in order that the old one might be finally put to rest.

One could view it as no more than a post-adolescent trauma. By this time in his life Francis has spent a year in a Perugian prison after Assisi's defeat by neighboring Perugia supporting Assisi's nobles.[1] He had attempted to join a crusade in southern Italy. At one point he had been placed in chains in his own house because of his bizarre behavior.[2] He had even tried to rebuild a ruined church by stealing his father's goods. All his actions seem disconnected, as if the young man was casting about for some direction to his life. Clearly the prospect of joining his father in the family business was less than enticing. Bedeviled by poetry, romantic ideas of chivalry, and a claustrophobic family environment, Francis had but one choice—to go off in search of his identity.

But this can only be a superficial view. His inner life was in turmoil. Something was happening that cannot be described in any pathological sense. If he were ill, then his symptoms were those of a man who had reached the end of his tether. In every way he was trying to come to terms with his destiny. He was trying to break the habits of a lifetime, those that directed him to living a normal life, a bourgeois life, and a life of a contented family man in Assisi. All his upbringing pressed him towards becoming a merchant, and so following in his father's footsteps. But something in him resisted this expectation. Francis, it seems to me, had already come to terms with the fact that he was different—and that he was, in some way, blessed.

I know these sound like remarks made in hindsight. His early biographers were good at that, too. In a place now known as Eremo delle Carceri, high on the mountain outside Assisi, Francis often used to retreat to a cave for days on end to wrestle with his furies. Today the place is a monastery where visitors are able to see the

---

1. The battle occurred in 1202. Francis was taken prisoner, and remained in Perugia until his father paid for his release.

2. According to Thomas of Celano, Francis was dragged from the street by his father and thrown into chains, before being shut away in a dark place for several days. This was done because he had embarrassed Pietro with a public display of madness and immoderation.

cave where he slept. On the path through the forest beyond the monastery there is a brass sculpture of Francis lying on his back, gazing up at the stars. It's said that he was fascinated with the constellations of Ursa Major and Ursa Minor, seeing in them the stellar orchestration of the names of his later orders, the Friars Majors and the Friars Minors.

"While his companion waited outside," wrote Thomas of Celano, "Francis, filled with a new and singular spirit, would pray to his Father in secret. He wanted no one to know what he did within….He prayed devoutly that the eternal and true God would direct his way, and teach him to do his will. He bore the greatest suffering in mind, and he was not able to rest until he should have completed in deed what he had conceived in heart….He was afire within himself with a divine fire, and he was not able to hide outwardly the ardor of his mind."

However strong these remarks might appear in hindsight, they nonetheless point to a more rigorous soul-searching than that which might occur in any other normal young man bent upon taking his place in the world. Clearly, Francis was no delinquent. Being filled "with a new and singular spirit" and not being able to conceal the "outward ardor of his mind" suggests that he was under some considerable stress. I will go so far as to say that Francis was experiencing a genuine spiritual crisis. His entire future depended upon whether he could resolve his fundamental conflict. That was, to abandon all expectations that others might have of him (including his father), and begin to live a new kind of life.

What was this life? One of absolute poverty. This is what impelled him to take all his possessions, including his horse, and sell them in Foligno. He wanted to be free of every impediment that might hinder the development of this "new and singular spirit" that possessed him. He wanted to do what Sören Kierkegaard expressed so succinctly: to live through, and experience the human in unparalleled intensity. More importantly perhaps, Francis wanted to strive to reinstate that primitive nature which he believed was his eternal origin. As Kierkegaard again remarked, he wanted to find a personality for whom the ethical preserves a sacred chastity…that in this life acquires the virgin purity of ethical passion, in comparison with which the purity of childhood is but an amiable jest.

When I speak of a primitive nature, I really mean a quality that inspires a recollection of what Kierkegaard calls the "eternal mark of the divinity" which releases a man from time. He is free then to embrace a life outside of the world-historical, outside the demands of society, outside even the more pressing demands of the body. Here we have the root of asceticism. A man must break free from history, from society, and from the singular presence of himself in order to begin the process of renewal. Further, he must fast from evil, as Empedocles suggests, and not seek intoxication in the astounding. All this is the makings of the ascetic, a person who is then able to discern magnitudes and transmute errors into something more substantial.

I suspect ideas similar to these were precisely what Francis was grappling with. Of course he had little or no knowledge of asceticism aside from what he had observed in normal daily life. Monks and flagellants were not an uncommon sight in medieval Italy, so he would have witnessed at least the more primitive techniques being employed, such as self-scourging and fasting. Probably he needed to come to terms with these rather grievous offerings anyway, if ever he was to become an ascetic. Was he prepared to live a life of abstinence, a life of celibacy, a life—in the end—of loneliness? These were surely some of the questions he must have asked himself at Carceri on those warm summer nights when it was easy to lie outside on the ground and look at the stars.

So the pressure was building. Francis had to make a choice. His attempts at avoiding the call had been at best misguided.

Riding off to Apulia, or trying to invest in a ruin, or making overtures to lepers—all these were no more than the gestures of someone who was floundering. He had not yet attained to that inwardness of spirit that would enable him to make a fundamental decision about himself: that he had no choice but to lead the life of a homeless ascetic, a celestial wanderer. What lay ahead for him was not the cloistered life of a monk, or the privileged preserve of a bishop, but that of a perpetual outsider. These issues formed the basis of the decision Francis had to make. He had to abandon every form of social construct, and every form of conventional religious routine, in order to realize a life that was in keeping with what he tentatively believed was his task, in spite of his indecision.

He was being called upon to develop a personality whose real identity was aligned with the utmost exertion of his powers. The hardest thing for him to do was to produce extraordinary effects in the external world, while knowing that in doing so, such gestures shouldn't engage his attention in any way. For he would have to accept that what he might achieve was not as a result of his power alone. He must therefore choose to remain in ignorance of what he might accomplish, so that his striving wouldn't be retarded by a preoccupation with externals. This ignorance would become the centerpiece of his personality, his accomplishment, and the exercise of his will. At the hour of his death he wouldn't even be aware that his life may have any significance other than that he had always striven to deny the yoke under which Brother Donkey had labored all his life—that of self-affirmation.[3]

It may be argued that not poverty but chastity represented

✳ ──────────

3. As Brother Giles remarked, perhaps echoing Francis's exhortation: "If a man were to live a thousand years and not have anything to do outside himself, he would have enough to do within, in his own heart, nor would he be able to bring the work to perfect completion—he would have so much to do only within, in his own heart!"

his biggest challenge. After all, he could always return to his father and ask forgiveness if things didn't work out. A life of celibacy, however, would force him to live outside the preserve of normal human relations, and put him at a distance from one of life's great impulses—that of experiencing family life. Celibacy, as we have already discovered, is a symbolic act of cessation, a kind of metaphor for suicide. When a man denies one of his fundamental urges he enters the domain of the neutered. To do so anchors him in a different kind of life. He is forever confined to that darkness of infertility, to the slopes of unsated desire.

At least this is how some people might view chastity. But for others, namely monks and clerics, chastity is no different than any other form of physical training. Whereas an athlete may push his or her body to extremes in order to realize a medal-winning performance, he or she does so in the knowledge that what might have been given up in order to achieve the objective makes it all worthwhile. Physical punishment is not an end in itself, but the means of achieving it. The satisfaction in winning, of breaking a record, celebrates a body honed to the point of absolute efficiency—and denial. It has done without so much in order to reach this point of perfection.

A monk would argue that he is bound by the same rules. As Brother Giles said: "It is impossible for a man to attain to grace unless he gives up sensuality." He didn't say that sensuality was evil; all he said was that if one wanted to achieve a state of grace, then something had to give. He even made a colorful allusion: "He who wishes to move big rocks and large beams tries to move them more by skill than by strength. We must proceed in the same way." In other words, chastity is a *skill*. It can only be acquired by careful attention to the task at hand. For a monk, chastity is like a clear mirror; it can be obscured just by breathing on it.

To choose celibacy, therefore, Francis knew what he was asking of himself. Chastity could only be an act of embellishment of the physical aspect of his being. He had to put himself into training for the greatest prize of all—that state of heightened grace that, many years later, he was to find at La Verna. Of course he wouldn't have known then what to expect from embracing a life of celibacy. All he would have been familiar with were the normal injunctions of ascetics the world over—that sensual restraint can lead to profound new insights into the working of the human spirit.[4] This choice was enough for the young man. Francis added chastity to his belt, along with holy poverty. The suffering and need for resolution that he'd experienced at Carceri on those lonely summer nights could only be achieved by some deep and incomparable commitment. He would have to give up the life of the senses, break in Brother Donkey to harness, and "farm the land that had not been farmed for a long time."

But obedience, the last of his vows, had yet to be acknowledged. In a sense, his whole life up to this point had been one of *dis*-obedience. As a somewhat dissolute man about town, a failed soldier, a would-be crusader, and an unsuccessful merchant, Francis bore all the hallmarks of someone who found any form of discipline abhorrent. Even to obey his father was guaranteed to provoke in him one form of outburst or another. It's not for nothing that he disappeared into some hole, or cave, where he often stayed for weeks in order to escape—or deny—his father's displeasure. One gets the feeling that Francis was in constant conflict with Pietro Bernardone because he simply refused to obey him. More than anything he wanted to stand up for a life that was independent of his father's expectations.

To embrace obedience as his final vow Francis needed to act

---

4. To the doubters of the value of chastity, Brother Giles had his answer: "Tanners know about skins, shoemakers about shoes, smiths about iron, and so on in other crafts. But how can a man know a craft he has never practiced? Do you think that great lords give great gifts to stupid and insane men? They do not."

in a way that demonstrated a supreme disobedience. He needed to create a disruption in the community that would finally put an end to his relationship with the world. Nothing less than an absolute rejection of his past and his perceived future would be sufficient. Deep inside, Francis may have wanted to enact Christ's walk in the Garden of Gethsemane shortly before his betrayal. He may have wanted to stand in the presence of God and prepare himself for his own encounter with denial. There was nothing for him to do but stand before those who had helped to make him what he was—his friends, his family, and the city fathers— and finally renounce all their claims upon him.

What happened next, on that April day, turned out to be one of the most significant events in the spiritual growth of Europe. A young man chose to defy his father publicly, and so rang out the death knell on filial piety. Until this point, at least the appearance of medieval hierarchy seemed to be intact: the father of the house received due respect from all those who lived in it, just as God the Father received reverence and homage from the great family of believers in his House. But when, on that early spring day, his father hauled Francis before the bishop to answer charges of theft, an act of defiance was precipitated that still reverberates down the centuries.

Thomas of Celano gives us a vivid account of the great act of disrobing which occurred on the steps of the bishop's palace in Assisi. In fact, he suggests that both father and son were implicated in a shadow play. Each was urging the other into making a more extreme gesture of rebuttal, as if each wanted to prove, once and for all, who was in the ascendant. As Thomas relates: "He then brought his son before the bishop of the city so that, renouncing all his possessions into his hands [that is, Pietro's], Francis might give up everything he had. Francis *not only did not refuse to do this,* but hastened with great joy to do what was demanded of him. Before the bishop he suffered no delay or hesitation, nor did he wait for any words, nor did he say anything. Instead Francis took off his clothes, bundled them together, and formally presented them to his father. He stripped himself completely naked."[5]

Giotto, that great thirteenth-century painter and precursor of the Renaissance, took the trouble to paint this scene in the basilica of San Francesco, in Assisi. We see Francis wrapped in a mantle held about his waist by Bishop Guido. To his left stands his father, Pietro Bernardone, whose arms are full of discarded clothing. He is gazing at his son with a look of fury. At the same time a friend, concerned that he may be about to hit his son, is holding him back. One senses a tremendous tension between the two men. Father and son are playing out the final act in their relationship. Between them social acceptance and spiritual anarchy are firmly pitted against each other. What we are seeing is the death of the old order, for Francis has made his statement: that nudity is his only defense against a society that cloaks everything in the objects of material status, class, guild affiliations, and the collectivity of belief. Even the Church was a party to this convention, since it, too, was firmly entrenched in the status quo. For all its occasional displays of incohesion, medievalism placed belief and the importance of social identity above that of the individual.

✳ ————————

5. It is interesting to note that Francis often used the act of nudity as a way of shocking his own followers into realizing their potential. It is recorded in *The Little Flowers of Saint Francis* how Brother Rufino, one of his closest friends, was asked by him to take off his clothes and preach in a church in Assisi, in order to overcome his reluctance to speak in public. Doing as he was ordered, Rufino, by his obedience, provoked Francis into following him. "How can you, Francis, you vile little wretch," he said of himself, "order Brother Rufino to go naked and preach to the people like a madman? By God, I am going to see that you do what you order others to do!" Francis then took off his habit and walked to Assisi naked, accompanied by Brother Leo, who discreetly carried along his and Brother Rufino's habit. On another occasion, he made a brother walk several miles naked in the cold and deep snow because he had disobeyed him.

What Francis achieved when he tossed aside his clothes that day was to cast off its stifling constraints for good.

Without realizing it, perhaps, Giotto had painted an act of rebellion. By stripping himself naked, Francis had made his position quite clear to all. Nothing in this world could humiliate him more than his own actions. Nor did anyone, not even his father, have any power over him. He had returned to his father his goods, his position, his identity, and any claims the man might wish to make on him. Francis was now a free man. There is a remark made in one of the Nag Hammadi gospels, which offers us a non-canonical but nonetheless interesting insight, which perfectly reflects what might have been going through Francis's mind during these moments: "Jesus said: 'When you disrobe without being ashamed, and take up your garments, and place them under your feet like little children, and tread on them, then will you see the son of the living one, and you will not be afraid.'" Francis, it seems, had finally renounced his fear of fear.

It is a significant moment. We are aware that Francis has embarked on a course from which there was to be no return. To go naked into the world is to renounce all its fabrications, all its pretense, and all its belief in the purely fortuitous act of worldly acceptance. A man who goes literally and figuratively naked takes upon himself a unique responsibility, for he is placing himself between man as a figure of concealment, of selfhood, and the mysterious perturbations of the Invisible. This is the chasm Francis crossed that day in Assisi, just as he was to cross that chasm at La Verna in order to receive the Stigmata years later. Nudity was the log over which he climbed to place himself in a condition of complete acceptance. His destiny now was in the hands of God.

It is interesting that Giotto should have invested so much of himself as an artist in painting the life of Francis. Historians agree that in these frescoes Giotto paved the way for the birth of humanism in Italian art. What they do not say is that Giotto seemed to have identified personally with Francis. After all, he was a near contemporary, born little more than forty years after Francis had died. I suspect that Francis's example, his willingness to defy society's conventions, helped Giotto to view his subject in a new way. What he painted in all the various tableaux on the walls of the basilica of San Francesco is a man whose grace was tempered by a rigorous and not unworldly inwardness. In Giotto's hands, Francis became the first man to stand apart in Western painting. In that sense Giotto celebrated the individual for the first time. The psychology of Francis interested him more than the ritual gestures that until then made up the subject and themes of medieval art.

Where could Francis go now that he had severed all connections with his native Assisi? His father had turned his back on him; the bishop, while sympathizing with his motives, had no use for him; his mother, Pica, whether she was on hand or not to witness this scene of mental and physical emasculation, had clearly abandoned him. He had no alternative but to leave Assisi and make his way north to Gubbio where he is said to have had friends. Thus, this man who had defied convention found himself cast adrift in a wild countryside. He took to the road, alone and half mad because of the stress of what had happened, knowing that he must somehow regain control of himself. Those who passed him on the track recall with some surprise, and not a little confusion, that he sang out aloud and in French like a man demented. It seems that a foreign language, the language of the outsider and of the troubadours had become his only companion.

Before he had reached the abbey of Valfabbrica near the Chiasicio River, he was dealt another blow. A band of robbers accosted him as he walked, and demanded to know who he was. It is at this moment that we begin to comprehend the full depth of the trauma that he had so recently experienced. The young man of the revels, the Perugian prisoner of war, the apprentice cloth-merchant wandering the roads of Provençe, this man had been put aside forever. The Francis of old had been extinguished. What stood before these robbers was a starker, a man in league with the Invisible. To their threats Francis simply replied in a loud and confident voice—in the voice of a man who had nothing to lose: "I'm the herald of the Great King. Why should you ask?" No wonder the thieves went crazy, stripped him once more, and threw him into a ditch. To contend with a man as disreputable as themselves, who also claimed to be the emperor's herald, struck them as an absurdity. He, like them, could only be a squire of the devil.

I decided to visit the abbey of Valfabbrica where Francis had spent his first days as an exile. It seemed to me that while other places sheltered his aspiration and his suffering, this abbey was the first place where he would have stayed in the wake of his decision to give up the world. Here he would have felt most alone. No one, not even the Church, had taken him in. He would have arrived at the gates of the monastery, disheveled, bruised, and without a friend in the world, knowing that he had nowhere to go. He had become, in the true sense, a supplicant. Yet when he arrived the monks treated him like a tramp. He was put to work in the kitchen as a scullion for a few days.

I eventually found the abbey down by the cemetery outside of town. The residential part of the building, or what is left of it, had been turned into a house. The ancient church, however, was still there, though locked up in the wake of a recent earthquake. After discussions with the householder, I drove back to town to find the local priest and request the key. Dom Gianfranco Castagnoli, a kindly man with time on his hands, agreed to accompany me back to Santa Maria Assunta and open the doors. When I entered the gutted church, I immediately felt the saint's presence. He was there, watching over the few remaining frescoes on the walls. In spite of his treatment by monks in an earlier age, he had somehow risen above their lack of charity and imposed his own sense of the sacred on the place.

Dom Gianfranco directed my attention to a large fresco of the Deposition of Christ, executed by the school of Cimabue (thirteenth century). It was a remarkable painting. The dead Christ was lying horizontally on a bed adorned by a winding sheet of complex and vivid patterns. Yet his figure was curiously devoid of any sign of pain. There was a calm about his expression, as if his mind had earlier detached itself from the anguish his body must have endured, and was now engaged in meditation upon the state of death. I couldn't help but recall Empedocles's haunting remark in this respect: "There was no discord and no unseemly strife in his limbs."

The figure made me think of Francis. He too had subjected himself to a crucifixion. He had found himself laid out on a rack. The figure of the Deposed Christ was a reflection of how he might have felt when he ate his meager scraps so reluctantly given to him by the monks at Valfabbrica. Finally, he understood what it was to be denied, to be scourged, and to be cast into a tomb of utter rejection. Yet, strangely, he had learned how to renounce himself. There was nothing left of him save an inner motion of the spirit. He had reached a point where he must learn how to maintain what little inner solitude he had achieved. This was all that the world had left him with: the strength, and the courage, to build up his own sense of inner freedom.

Somehow I could see in the Christ figure lying at peace within the sumptuous oriental space of the fresco intimations of this new kind of man that Francis wanted to become. He alone was struggling with the dilemma of how to become the "herald of the Great King." He alone was preparing himself for the moment when he might transform his age. Of course, all this was in the future, and his immediate preoccupation would have been with survival. Nonetheless, what he would discover in the years ahead would serve as one of the fundamental tenets of freedom. He would learn how to trust.

I quit the church of Santa Maria Assunta with Dom Gianfranco, and together we walked out into the chill air of early winter. I think we were both conscious of having witnessed an ancient agony, yet one that still retained its message of renewal. Nor did it detract from something else we both shared: that together we were heirs to one of history's great acts of rebellion. Francis had set us on a course that would take us away from ourselves. Meister Eckhart spoke of this as the only free possession that we can retain.

CHAPTER FOUR

The Voice
of the Crucifix

✳

D o we have a description of Francis? Thomas of Celano attempted to record the impressions of those who had known him during his lifetime. We observe a short man in stature, with a moderately sized head and elongated face. He possesses a forehead that is smooth and low. He has black hair, a straight nose, and smallish ears that protrude from the side of his head. A later portrait by Cimabue in the basilica of San Francesco shows a similarity in appearance, except that now his hair is tonsured and he wears a thin beard. Giotto retains this image of the saint in his frescoes, while adding to his face a certain spiritual rigor and insight. So physically he is not unknown to us. We are looking at a man of medium height, slender, with small feet and skinny legs.[1]

✳ ────────

1. In St. Gregory's Chapel in the monastery of Subiaco, there is a fresco depicting Francis without a halo, and without the wounds of the Stigmata on his hands. It is likely that this painting was painted before his death, and before he had received the Stigmata. We see a similar portrait as of those referred to in the text.

It's important that we know what sort of man we are dealing with. He was no Amazon, in spite of his zest for long treks even in the harshest weather. Sometimes we forget how far it is to Spain from Umbria—and to think that he walked there without considering the physical difficulties. Now that I have visited many of the places associated with his life I can testify to the challenge the location of some of these remote sanctuaries must have posed. Umbria is mountainous, it is wild even today. The smallest towns are built on high knolls behind forbidding walls, so that to climb there at the end of a day must have been extremely fatiguing. In winter, too, it can be very cold: snow often covers the land, bleeding it white. Francis and his followers must have balked at times when they viewed the weather outside, before beginning their long march to some other hamlet along the road.

Yet it is a land of sweet melancholy. You only have to peer into the paintings of Umbrian artists like Perugino, Gentile da Fabriano, and Benedetto Bonfigli to see how deeply attached people were in those days to tree-clad hills, contorted vaults of stone, and garden seats overgrown with vine. I sense a wistfulness at work in the mind of these artists: they were forever trying to capture something that they felt was there, hovering between appearance and non-appearance, that slowly revealing image of nature in some way attempting to contemplate itself. To the Umbrian artist, this form of meditation was the supreme act of communication. These artists perhaps wanted Umbria to reflect an often strongly felt belief that the earth may have been an angel in disguise.

It's no accident that Umbrian artists liked to paint their Madonna and Infant portraits in the countryside, rather than in an enclosed architectural background so favored by Florentine artists. I think they believed that the Virgin would feel more at ease seated among rocks, trees, and flower-decked gardens than in some regal boudoir in town. She was only the wife of a carpenter after all, not that of a prince. Hers was the landscape of nature, the hard, stony environment of Palestine, the sandy riverbanks of the Nile to where she and Joseph had escaped from the agents of Herod.

Francis was born into these mountains with their seasonal pasture, their rubbled riverbeds and upland forests. In his youth he had possibly shared a meal with farmers around their hearths. He had probably watched sword smiths at work over their forge, hammering out instruments of war. He understood the intricacy of harness-making, and the storage of the harvest against winter's dearth. Probably on occasions he had even joined in olive-picking, and helped bring in the grapes after the first thunderstorms at the beginning of autumn. Thus he was a man of his place and his time, constrained by their limitations, yet still able to draw strength from their enduring covenant with the countryside of Umbria.

To visit such places and gaze back through time is to enter the landscape of these Umbrian artists. I felt strongly, however, that I wasn't looking back at Francis's life, but observing it as it unfolded. I had tramped the back road to Gubbio and kept an eye out for wolves; I had climbed through the forest to the hill of La Verna; I had sat in his tiny cell outside Cortona and contemplated the marks in the wall that he had gouged with his bare hands; I had presented myself in the square of Alviano where Francis had once reprimanded the swallows. Umbria, for all its remoteness, for all its introversion, is still a familiar place. It is as if, by following in his footsteps, I have been able to view it as he might—as a place where the mind can abjure all its terrors when confronted with the smile of a tree.

San Damiano, now a small monastery located on the slope below Assisi, is where Francis's great adventure began. It was this building that precipitated his break with his father; it was here, too, that he had received a message from God. An ancient crucifix on the wall there was a witness to this conversation, since it was through the wounded Christ that Francis received his first directive: "Repair my house. As you see, it is falling into ruin." That crucifix, in painted wood, still hangs above the altar where Francis first saw it. Viewing this joyous image of Christ Crucified, I began to sense that the painting may yet act as a microphone for the voice of God, should he decide to make some new pronouncement.[2]

Thomas of Celano maintained that Francis didn't rebuild the church from the ground up, but rather that he "repaired it zealously." Since the money he had originally hoped to finance this enterprise with was returned to his father at the time of their breakup, Francis found himself in a dilemma. If he were to carry out his dream, then he would have to rebuild the church with his own hands. He was able to do this by begging stones and building material from the people of Assisi. In return for their generosity he promised people a "reward from the Lord." Already, it seems, he was dealing with a new kind of currency. Poverty may have limited his spending power, but it hadn't prevented him from rebuilding San Damiano. It was a first step in devising a new way of life for himself—a life that was no longer dependent upon money.

Initially I found it hard to understand Francis's abhorrence of money. There was nothing in his early life that might have suggested why he should be so fanatical in his distaste for it. But

---

2. I am reminded here by what the Persian Illuminist philosopher Suhrawardi (1153–1191), a near contemporary of Francis (1182–1226), said in this respect: "Supra-sensory realities encountered by the prophets, the Initiates, and others appear to them sometimes in the form of lines of writing, sometimes in the hearing of a voice which may be gentle and sweet, and which can also be terrifying. Sometimes they see human forms of extreme beauty who speak to them in most beautiful words [that is, the seraph at La Verna] and converse with them intimately about the invisible world; at other times these forms appear to them like those delicate figures proceeding from the most refined work of the painters."

if one delves more deeply into his concept of poverty as his medium of exchange with the world, perhaps his attitude may appear more comprehensible. He saw poverty as an act of freeing himself from the fear of *loss*. Here is the key. Money implies possession that implies ownership. Owning things invokes the specter of responsibility to those things, and the need to expend energy protecting them. From Francis's viewpoint, it can only be a wasted energy since it is tied to the inertia of objects and their corresponding drift toward deterioration. A life dedicated to the preservation of material objects, whether they be a house, a business, possessions, or a country estate demands a certain kind of commitment that draws a person away from the real business at hand—that of the cultivation of the spirit.

Francis saw the danger clearly. Something in his makeup, a kind of poetry of dispossession, allowed him to see the flaws in medieval society. The rise of the merchant class in towns like Florence, Siena, Assisi, and Perugia was slowly eroding the old aristocratic ideal. It may even be argued that the penchant for mounting crusades at this time was an attempt by popes, kings, and nobles to divert attention away from the dismantling of a society that was still firmly entrenched in the principle of hierarchy. The merchant class however was more egalitarian, less dependent on family lineage, and more eager to dismiss those closed networks of city-states, bedeviled as they were by internecine feuds. If a man like Bernardone could travel to France and do business with his counterparts, without invoking the need to make either territorial claims or a marriage alliance, then surely his presence in the medieval equation was potentially disruptive. In his hands, a shipload of cotton from Flanders held more cachet in the market of Assisi or Foligno than a dozen well-armed knights on route to Acre or Jerusalem to defend some outmoded aristocratic ideal.

Francis, for all his devotion to the old chivalric ways, as well as his background as a merchant's son, embodied this conflict perfectly. On the one hand he wanted to ride off to Palestine and perform feats of heroism; on the other, he was quite happy to sell goods in Spello or Rieti at a profit. He knew the value of cloth. I suspect that knowledge of both these worlds helped him to understand the real nature of commercial exploitation. The nobles' values were founded upon prodigality, consanguinity, and the ownership of vast estates; the merchant's upon frugality, mutuality, and the amassing of capital. The former might be represented by Frederick II of Sicily who dominated his kingdom by force of arms and diplomatic panache; the latter, by a man like Cosimo de Medici, the first flower of Florentine commerce.

Writing much later, but still about issues close to a merchant's heart in the thirteenth century, the philosopher Leon Battista maintained that no one who was poor "would find it easy to acquire honor and fame by means of his virtues"; that poverty "threw virtue into shadows," and subjected it to "hidden and obscure misery." Matteo Palmieri, another Florentine philosopher of old merchant stock, agreed with this view. In his opinion only the successful merchant who traded on a large scale was worthy of regard or honor. Gregorio Dati, one of Florence's international silk merchants, went so far as to say: "A Florentine who is not a merchant, who has not traveled through the world, seeing foreign nations and peoples, and then returned to Florence with some wealth, is a man who enjoys no esteem whatsoever." While these men were voicing their opinions more than a hundred years after men like Pietro Bernardone took ship for France or walked across the Alps, the substance of their remarks would have found favor with the Assisian merchant. He too would have regarded his commercial success as "worthy of regard," and that his riches were no less than "comely and grand." It was precisely such pretensions that might have stimulated Francis into considering medieval commerce for what it was: a progressive materialization of the collective spirit of the age, which in time paved the way for the rise of secularism during the fifteenth century. It is arguable that the Renaissance could not have happened in Italy without the support of the merchant class of Florence, nor in England without the commercial benefits that accrued as a result of the feats by privateers like Drake and Hawkins on the Spanish Main.

Of course Francis wouldn't have been aware of the historical processes at work during his day. But he would have been conscious that things were changing. His father's dedication to commerce, and pride in his own success, may well have touched a sore spot in Francis. As an outsider, one who more than ever found himself the brunt of ridicule in Assisi, he could see what others were blind to: that of the growth of a dismissive urge by wealthy people toward poverty and issues of the spirit. Piety is one thing—and rich people are the first to attend church—but losing contact with that deep current of religiosity that had made Italy such a civilized haven was turning its people into squirrels. Prudence and possessions were taking the place of simple, unadorned belief.

Francis's championing of poverty was not so much a desire to live as the poor might (although that was implicit), but to strip himself of all attachments. He recognized that in his previous life he had been chained to these. Wealth, family, social position, profession—all of them confined him in a web of relationships which made it impossible to define himself as a full human being in the image of Christ. By stripping himself of his clothing he had made a potent act of rejection: everything must be given up if one were to wield a sword against a life of entanglement. The inner person must be brought to the fore again rather than continue to remain cloaked in costly silks and velvet.

Francis's gesture was no different to that of the yogi in India, or the wandering dervish in Arabia. These visionaries had embraced a life determined by what, in Greek, is known as *enthymios*. That is, the act of meditating, conceiving, imagining, and projecting with the full force of the heart and mind upon the object of one's desire. It's not surprising that a painted wooden image in a ruined church "spoke" to Francis. For he had already made himself open to the suggestive, indeed, magical nature of the image as a repository of spirit. It may be said that he bore the consciousness of God's words within his breast, and projected them onto the crucifix. Either way, it was a miracle: the image of Christ on the cross endowed his thoughts with a creative potency that demanded action. "Rebuild my church," was both the remark of God *and* Francis, to himself.

All gesture is an act of communication, a visual language. One must not see Francis's behavior as bizarre or out of sorts, but as the syntax of some deeper form of expression. Of course bizarre behavior is unnerving because it is disruptive. Walking naked through the street, or demanding a friend to place his foot on his head and then walk down his body,[3] or punishing a brother for touching money,[4] these are extreme acts. Francis didn't resort to them because he was mad, but because he realized early that

---

❊ ———————

3. At Carceri on one occasion, Francis's good friend Bernard of Quintavalle was in retreat. When the man hadn't acknowledged his calls from the track below, Francis grew impatient. Later, when the two finally met, Francis was filled with remorse when he learned from Bernard that he hadn't heard his calls because he was so deep in prayer and meditation. "I command you," he said to Bernard, "to punish my presumption and the insolence of my heart. As soon as I lie down on my back, you shall put one foot on my throat and the other on my mouth, and then you shall walk on top of me three times...."

❊ ———————

4. Francis was always condemning his followers for touching money. In one case, he argued that money should be regarded as dung. Thomas of Celano relates: "It happened one day that a certain secular person entered a church to pray, and he left some money as an offering. When he had gone, one of the brothers simply touched the money with his hand and threw it on the window sill. Francis heard what the brother had done; and the brother, realizing that he had been found out, hurried to ask for pardon. Francis upbraided the brother, and commanded the man to lift the money from the window sill with his mouth, and place it on the asses' dung outside."

reasonable discourse wouldn't have the same effect. Deep inside he knew that people longed to be shocked.

The idea of poverty for Francis became a concerted act of sacrifice. He wanted to show that it was possible to give up everything, to free oneself from the world. One shouldn't confuse this with being poor, which is not a free act, but one imposed from outside. That Francis chose a condition associated with human despair may be likened to that of Christ freely choosing death. Poverty became Francis's martyrdom, his Calvary, his chariot of fire. Like Buddha under the Bodhi Tree renouncing all karmic life, poverty for Francis was his Great Refusal—or indeed his Great Acceptance.

I am reminded of Christ's remark in this respect: "Blessed are the poor in spirit for they shall enter the kingdom of heaven." It is clear that Christ meant more than embracing a life of lack, or destitution, as a means to an end. I think his message was that those who have a more profound understanding of their spiritual poverty are only able to break free from their condition by embracing a life of detachment. All Francis did was follow in the footsteps of certain bodhisattvas of Japan who often adopted extreme modes of behavior in order to unlock aspects of their sensibility. In this sense, poverty becomes a key to a higher level of understanding and self-abandonment.

Poverty was a way of stepping outside the conventions of human discourse. Francis instinctively knew that his vision for humankind couldn't be expressed in any other way than by a strong allegiance to poverty. For him it was almost an act of sedition, as it called into question the whole premise of society. To do so was to begin to rebuild it from the inside. It was this distinction that Francis tried to instill into his followers. His actions were often extreme for no other reason than, like any revolutionary teacher, he was trying to shock people out of their habitual thought patterns. He wanted them to confront hunger, failure, rejection, and the loss of fraternity, ill-health, hardship, isolation, and exile—all these so-called negative values—in a bid to overturn the facile imperatives of his time.

For Francis may have seen the kingdom of heaven not as a place, however otherworldly, but as a state of mind. He may have regarded it as a Zen Buddhist might—as a state of *satori,* or even Nirvana. Many Christians do not like to think of their religion as the repository of ecstatic experiences, unless they are associated with deeply emotional religious events. But when one talks of "bliss," it is no more than an acknowledgment of reaching a state of understanding of the Eternal Nature. Bliss allows one to glimpse the primary foundations of the kingdom of heaven—that is, the final severance of humankind from time. Understanding this condition is to enter a state of "bliss."

Thomas of Celano relates a story about Brother Giles, one of the founding members of the Franciscan brotherhood. He tells of how King Louis of France visited the friar during his pilgrimage to the Holy Land. The two men met, embraced, and said not a word to one another. When asked later by his followers why they hadn't conversed, Brother Giles replied:

DO NOT BE SURPRISED *that neither he nor I was able to say anything to each other. In that moment when we embraced, the light of divine wisdom revealed his heart to me and mine to him. We heard without sound made by lips or tongue even better than if we had spoken with our lips. For if we had wanted to explain with the help of our voices what we felt in our hearts, because of the defect in language, which cannot clearly express the secret mysteries of God except by mystic symbols, that conversation would have saddened rather than consoled us.*

✳

This statement is a remarkable admission because it tells us a lot about the inner nature of these men. King and humble monk met on the field of understanding. They had both, in their own way, achieved a state of bliss. What they had experienced was *unutterable.* Through them the Divine revealed Himself to Himself by differentiating Himself in their respective being. They became absorbed into something far greater than themselves.

Another brother who followed in Francis's footsteps, John of La Verna (1259–1322), was a man who achieved a state of bliss while living as a recluse at La Verna. It was said of him that "he was raised to such a marvelous light in God that he saw in the Creator all created things, both in heaven and on earth, all disposed in their various realms....Afterwards God raised him above every creature so that his soul was absorbed and assumed into the abyss of the Divinity and Light, and it was buried in the ocean of God's Eternity and Infinity, to the point where he could not feel anything that was created or formed or finite or conceivable or visible which the human heart could conceive or the tongue describe." Later, when he had meditated upon what had happened, Brother John "came to unutterable insights" which informed him that only through Christ could everlasting life be achieved.

This "ocean of Eternity and Infinity" is a fitting way to describe what those like Francis were committed to understanding. They were true adventurers of the spirit whose destination was always going to be that of ecstatic experience. Poverty, chastity, and trusting self-sufficiency were all part of the discipline that they applied to themselves, knowing that in doing so they were perhaps preparing their minds and spirits for a visitation by the seraph. Descriptions of John of La Verna's experiences, or those of Francis himself, should not surprise us. They are the product of a careful application of mind over matter, the thoughtful and resolute attempt at dematerializing the visible world in pursuit of something more rarefied.

All this may sound outlandish in an age of computer wizardry. But in Francis's day, communication with the other world was not a technological event. It was something that happened only after a prolonged association with those emanations that pervaded what was then considered to be the "ether." The ether was formally believed to be a rarefied and highly elastic substance that permeated all space, including the interstices between particles of matter. It gave rise to the idea of the ethereal, which described an impalpable, unearthly delicacy and refinement of the spirit. To tap into this wasn't an impossible dream. All it required was a "change of heart" in the recipient for the primordial cloud to open and offer up its secrets.

I suspect this is what happened to Francis when he first set eyes on the crucifix at San Damiano. All his experiences coalesced in what he saw hanging in the apse of the church. The Crucifixion represented a cosmic rupture in the old order; and God's injunction to rebuild the church was a voice out of the primordial depths of this rupture. Francis, primitive that he was, wanted to bear the burden of this rupture and make it the core of his life. He wanted to bear *crucificial being* upon his shoulders, and so duplicate the event as a continuing one. Few had attempted this task before him; fewer still were ever going to follow him on his journey into the dark night of the soul. But one must understand the process: it is that of a person who was in flight from the ordinary, from that which makes a man less than he is, from those conditions that denied faith its unity of will and action. Francis had stamped himself with the mark of Cain so that he might cleanse his age.

In the courtyard of San Damiano, I was made conscious of the battle Francis had waged in defense of what he believed to be the new dispensation. It was here that he had heard the voice of God issuing from a crucifix. It was here, too, that during the last year of his life, when he was physically broken and in the care of the one he loved most, Clare di Offreduccio, that he composed his *Canticle of Brother Sun,* his paean to the world that he had resisted, embraced, and endured. Below, in the church itself, the crucifix still hangs above the altar, a testimony to that voice. As I've remarked before, it doesn't depict Christ in agony. Instead, it is the figure of God suspended in ether, sublimely suffering for the love of humankind. One senses that this tiny church has witnessed some memorable events, events that have their origin in a young man's desire to rebuild a ruin and so augment his own faith.

Why did I come here? I asked myself. To gaze upon that crucifix? Or simply to recall those days when Francis broke stones and mortared walls? I can see him now, his hair filled with stone dust, warmly accepting roof beams and other building materials from those who stopped by to watch him at work. People were fascinated. For all their reserve, many sensed that they were witnessing more than just the rebuilding of a ruined chapel. San Damiano was the start of something. The naked warrior from their home town was now actively employed at last. Perhaps he would return to the fold. Perhaps he would abandon the life of a mendicant and reclaim his rightful place in the bosom of his family.

These dreams of normality have a hollow ring about them. I knew that Francis would never have settled for such a life. He was committed to rebuilding more than a church; what he wanted to do was renovate a whole way of thinking. For him San Damiano was an *omphalos,* a world center no different to Delphi in ancient Greece or Benares in India. He wanted it to stand for something that would continue to be important long after he had passed on. The crucifix suspended in the chapel was the living embodiment of a voice that would never fade away so long as human beings believed in supernatural realities, in their right to have some contact with the Invisible.

CHAPTER FIVE

Clare's Tryst

✳

O n a wall of the lower basilica of San Francesco in Assisi there is a fresco painted by Simone Martini. It depicts a young woman with an aquiline face, slender nose, and small mouth. Her forehead and hair are draped in a white cowl that is crossed loosely over one shoulder. Beneath her habit there is sense of a young woman in the pride of youth. Her gaze, however, is turned inward. She is not looking at the viewer, but rather is exploring some distant image out of frame. Behind her head is a large, intricately designed mandala made up of the heads of cherubim and rosettes. Beyond the halo itself lies a purple mist of paint that suggests an ocean of depth and restraint.

When I compare it to another painting in the basilica of Santa Chiara nearby I am struck by the similarity in appearance.[1] Clare's expression is dominated by the same absence of eye contact. Obviously she was a woman who found it difficult to gaze directly upon another. It could have been shyness on her part, of course.

✳ ─────────

1. This phenomenon can also be viewed in another painting by Simone Martini, alongside that of one of Francis, in the same basilica. In this painting, Clare is seen gazing out of frame. As an iconic gesture it suggests a woman who has known what troubadours called *fin' amor*, a distant love.

But, knowing her strength of character and her stubbornness, I begin to think that what I am looking at is a woman who had grown up harboring a secret. She was a woman who, quite early in life, had recognized something in herself that could not be reached either by filial affection, friendship, or human love. It was not coldness that characterized her demeanor so much as a sense of unreachable solitude. Clare di Offreduccio, it seems to me, was one of those rare people who harbors what might be called a transcendent intuition, a knowledge of God.

Why do I say this? All the reports of Clare suggest a young woman who fell in love with Francis at a tender age. Her infatuation for him was determined as much by her own youthful embrace of life as the sheer audacity of his recent behavior in the streets of Assisi. Here was a young girl, barely seventeen while he was nearing thirty, who had the temerity to recognize in his inversion of values, his willful lack of conformity, something with which she could immediately identify. It was not love in the sense of a strong physical attraction that she experienced, but love in the sense of someone who had been seduced by an apparitional figure. This figure, in the person of Francis, embodied an angelic function and secured for her confirmation that there might exist a sympathy between the invisible and the visible, the spiritual and the sensible.

It is no mean feat. But then, Francis had already shown himself to be a person who, at the court of values, was not afraid to devise his own. By casting himself adrift from the laws of social probity and acceptability, he had set a course into unknown seas. This made his voyage, to a detached eye anyway, appear dangerous. Like the seafarers of his day, he could be risking death by sailing beyond Cape Bojador on the far west coast of Africa, then believed to be the place where the world disc came to an abrupt end. His behavior might prove to be an invitation to plunge into the abyss. It might also prove to be extremely alluring.

Until this point in her life, Clare had lived the normal existence of a child from a wealthy family. Unfortunately, because of the disruption caused by the war between Assisi and Perugia, she had spent most of her early years away from the family home. The noble families were not much liked in Assisi during this period of social conflict, so it was prudent for her father and mother to remove the household to Perugia. There she had grown up in a protected environment, the daughter of an exile, and so, in a sense, tolerated by the people of Perugia. She probably knew that at least some of her fellow Assisians were incarcerated in the dungeons below the city during this time, but it is unlikely that Francis Bernardone's name ever cropped up in conversation. He was just another prisoner, and she the daughter of one of his oppressors.

Inevitably, through social standing and class alone, there was a gap between them. Moreover, the added burden of exile must have lent a touch of poignancy to a young girl's dream about home. Though she was only seventeen years old, marriage was nonetheless a real option for a family long used to marriage contracts and alliances. Perhaps, among fellow aristocratic exiles in Perugia, there was a man already picked out to wed her when the time was right. Clare's destiny seemed clear: her beauty, that calm detachment which precluded all but a solitary distance, would be betrothed to a young man well able to claim her marriage dowry as an adjunct to his own wealth.

So what happened to change this prospect? It was a question that I often asked myself on the occasions when I walked the streets of Assisi or stepped into the basilica of Santa Chiara to gaze at her mummified body in its gilded casket behind glass. Distance and death had not made her any more approachable. She lay there in her black habit, her head swathed in white, a bunch of plastic lilies in her hands, still gazing towards some distant place. Now, of course, Assisi is a hodgepodge of tourist shops selling trinkets celebrating the memory of Francis and Clare. All these tokens can do is commemorate what is conventional about their relationship: that of two devout people who inspired one another into a deeper commitment to God. But I suspect what really happened had more to do with interior recognition than it did piety.

It's not easy to talk about a love between two people that doesn't conform to the normal demands of mutual attraction. In medieval times, if you took away the social and political fabric that cloaked marriage, there was still enough left over to inspire talk of emotions and a quickening of the heart. Courtly love had reached into Italy by way of the troubadours, and many ideas drawn from Moorish Spain had filtered through to the studies of the learned in Florence. Ibn Hazm, a Cordovan poet of the Ommayad period (eleventh century), could remark, "I see a human form, but when I meditate more thoroughly, I think I see in it a body that comes from the celestial world of the Spheres." He then went on to argue that "love, in and of itself, is an accident and therefore cannot be the basis of other accidents." This idea is echoed by Dante in almost the same words nearly three hundred years later: "Love does not exist in and of itself as a substance: it is the accident of a substance."[2] Ibn Hazm also goes on to quote Ibn Dawud, who in turn quotes from Plato's *Symposium:* "My opinion [on the nature of love] is that it consists of the union of the parts of souls that go about divided, by comparison with how they were at the beginning in their elevated essence." Plato's idea that souls seek each other out in the world because of the relationships they had before descend-

---

✳ ────────

2. Though nearly 300 years separate Ibn Hazm's remark made in a book known as *The Necklace of the Dove* (1022), and Dante's remark made in *La Vita Nuova,* it confirms what many scholars now believe: that Dante was deeply influ- enced by Islamic ideas derived from Spain, not least the work of Ibn Arabi (1165–1240), himself a contemporary of Francis. It is arguable that Dante's Mystic Rose is based upon the one Ibn Arabi described in one of his books.

ing to earth and assuming a body, is known as the doctrine of *reminiscence.*

Fin' amor, or a distant love, implicitly acknowledges the doctrine of reminiscence. But while it alerts us to the existence of other realities, those embodied in what Ibn Hazm calls the World of the Spheres, it is nonetheless grounded in a courtly eroticism. There is still something physical at work underneath the surface. A person may remember a sublime incident out of a previous life, but is never entirely removed from the physical demand made by love itself. So that a real tension exists—a tension that clearly enveloped Clare when she first set eyes on Francis.

No one really knows when this happened. More than likely it occurred after her return from exile to Assisi as a young woman, and after Francis was released from a Perugian jail. It may be that, during one of her chaperoned walks about town, she had noticed Francis's antics in the street when he went about begging. She would have recalled his reputation as a leader of the revels, too, and his subsequent renunciation of all his worldly goods. The contact would have struck her deeply: a young mind would have had difficulty grappling with such a dichotomy. A rich man chooses beggary; a young merchant abandons his store. Yet something about Francis's behavior must have touched her: a sense perhaps that the social disruption he was causing had its origin in a more profound disruption of the spirit.

Young people, at a critical point in their lives, are often open to influences that later they will dismiss. This point usually arrives when the critical faculty has been awakened and the innocence of youth has not yet been abased. It is a fragile moment. To inhabit this domain, for however long it lasts, can prove to be a life-determining event. Yet to experience the wonder and chaos of existence as an unfragmented whole can also unleash powerful contradictory emotions. A young man or woman may feel that they are being buffeted by a storm, that they have no skills to deal with the continuing presence of the uncanny. For that is what they are encountering: the uncanny, after all, is a coming-into-nearness of the primordial depths of existence. To deal with it is like dealing with a wild animal.

For two people to be experiencing such an emotion at the same time, and in the presence of one another, is to offer the world a potent human elixir. Ordinary things register in a different way; a strain of music may be experienced as something painfully beautiful, a line of poetry as saying something infinitely expressive, a field of flowers as a visual poem in itself. What is happening is both paradoxical and confusing; we are led astray by our emotions, our sensibilities and our feelings, and find ourselves unable to "come down to earth."

How does one deal with such an experience? One can either dismiss it entirely and succumb to the carnal. One can retreat into an ivory tower and allow extreme sensitivity to reign. Or one can recognize the full implication of what is happening and place oneself in the preserve of this transcendent intuition. I think the latter is what Clare did when she encountered Francis. She saw in him a person who embodied all that she was grappling with, for she, too, was being buffeted by religious questions of her own. Her longing was to know a world untrammeled by the baseness of politics, the daily problems at home, and her family's desire to see her well married. In a word, Clare was confused.

Could one say the same about Francis? He was older by twelve years and already committed to a life of mendicancy. All his recent actions were those of a man in league with a divine madness. He'd set himself up as Assisi's conscience, daring its inhabitants either to accept him or drive him out of town. Already others were beginning to embrace his cause. Brother Giles, Sabbatino, Morico, John della Capello, Philip the Long, Angelo Tancredi, Bernard of Quintavalle, Elias Buonbarone of Cortona, Juniper, Leo, Masseo of Marignano, Peter Catani, and Brother Rufino had also joined his fledgling brotherhood.[3] These men were living in a rough camp on the plain below Assisi, at a place known as Portiuncula.

Was Francis prepared to experience in the person of Clare an abiding sense of the other? The chronicles seem to think so—but always with the proviso that between them no physical intimacy occurred. Theirs was a love, so the story goes, made in Heaven. What they saw in one another is precisely what Ibn Hazm described: a recognition that they were souls who had been united in an earlier life, and who had found each other again in this one. It sounds like a romantic fiction. Yet this image of two "linked atoms" (*les atoms ecrochus*) eventually finding one another, and committing themselves to the same ideal, persists. In the process, they have joined other such luminaries as Abelard and Heloise, Tristan and Isolde, Paolo and Francesca, Dante and Beatrice. All these great trysts, of course, celebrate different aspects of the human condition. Moreover, what Francis and Clare's relationship brought to the human experiment was a shared realization in the transcendent value of radical poverty.

I suspect that Francis was powerfully attracted to Clare, judging by her various portraits. She was indeed a beauty. No man, however celibate he might think himself, could help but notice a woman in the full flower of her maidenhood—who at the same time radiated a certain detachment and coolness. Virginity can be an aphrodisiac, especially when it is accompanied by an untouchability that is almost provocative. Francis would have sensed this; he would have known, too, that he was dealing with

---

✳ ─────────

3. To the last, Francis always insisted on calling his congregation a brotherhood rather than an order. He felt that the latter term rigidified what was a natural calling. It was only after he gave up the post of Vicar General and wrote yet another rule toward the end of his life, that he conceded to the name change. By that time, he had withdrawn from the world and felt that his public duties were over. He had even abandoned the right to have personal friends, such was the distance that he had placed between himself and the world.

no ordinary woman. In Clare, he had met someone who was already in defiance of what she stood for, even if she did not know it yet. Such a condition only he understood, since he had begun to live a similar life himself.

So if we assume that Francis became in his own way infatuated by Clare, what was it that he experienced? I think he found himself caught up in a range of conflicting emotions. On one hand, he was grateful to have found a sympathetic ear to listen to his dreams and his hopes; on the other, he must have been conscious of the dangers he was opening himself up to. Love between the daughter of an aristocrat and a commoner was risky enough; but between a confessed celibate and a young virgin smacks of a heinous crime. Though it did not happen until seventy-five years later, the passion that erupted between Paolo and Francesca is symptomatic of how such a liaison would have been viewed in Francis's time.[4] To have besmirched the reputation of a young woman, a di Offreduccio no less, would have been dealt with severely by her family. Death would not be out of the question.

I suspect rather that Francis was forced to come to terms with his own emotions in his relationship with Clare. His youth must have been subject to a certain kind of torture, in spite of his professed belief in chastity. He would have gazed into those haunting eyes, eyes that had until then harbored only a solitary distance, wondering what he might be feeling and whether his dream

---

4. Dante alluded to the love between Paolo and Francesca in his *Divine Comedy*. There he placed the two lovers in Hell because they had contravened the marriage vow. It is a poignant story: Paolo was the brother of Francesca's husband, Gianciotto da Verrucchio, the deformed son of the lord of Rimini. The two of them were reading a story from the Arthurian legends when they chanced upon a description of Lancelot kissing King Arthur's queen, Guinevere. As they did so, their eyes met. Francesca's cheeks colored. Then they read of lips long-thwarted. Paolo then kissed Francesca and, according to Dante, they "read no more that day." The lovers were discovered together by Gianciotto who, in a fit of frenzy, stabbed them both to death.

was real. Again, he would have asked himself whether he possessed the courage to maintain his self-imposed vow. Clare represented the willfulness of beauty pressing towards its desired object: that coalescence of mind and body into one tumultuous act of heartfelt passion. Could he resist, or was he just another would-be ascetic concealing his real feelings under his habit?

Gazing at the withered body of Clare in the basilica of Santa Chiara, I couldn't help but ask these questions. It was not enough to see Francis as a man of superhuman willpower who despised the flesh, and who regarded women as less than equal. It is true that he distanced himself from them and advised his brothers to do so also, but this doesn't mean that he was a misogynist as has often been said of him. His dealings with women later in his life were characterized by a broad sympathy mingled with reserve. In Gubbio, he had no hesitation in giving back a woman her sight, and straightening the crippled hands of another. As Thomas of Celano relates: "When she learned that Francis had entered the city, she immediately ran to him;... she showed her crippled hands to him and began to ask him to touch them. Moved to pity he touched her and healed her. Immediately the woman went home full of joy, made a kind of cheesecake with her hands, and offered it to the holy man. He took a little of it in his kindness and commanded the woman to eat the rest of it with her family."[5]

✳ ─────────────

5. Thomas of Celano relates another moving story: "It happened in the winter that Francis was wearing a cloth folded after the manner of a mantle. ...An old woman came up to him begging alms. Immediately he loosened the cloth from his neck, and gave it to the poor woman, saying: 'Go, make yourself a dress, for you are greatly in need of one....' Quickly she ran away, and cut the cloth with her scissors. When she found the cut cloth would not be enough for a dress, she returned to the saint, indicating to him that it was not enough. Francis turned to a companion, who had the same kind of cloth on his back. 'Did you hear, Brother?' he said, 'what this poor woman said? Let us put up with the cold for the love of God and give the cloth to the old woman, so that she might complete her dress.' His companion did so, and both remained naked so that the old woman might be clothed."

The testimony is conflicting. There's a story told by Thomas of Celano, for example, of how Francis lowered his head as he thanked a mother and her daughter when they gave him food on his journey to Bevagna. When asked by a companion why he hadn't looked such gentle people in the face, he replied: "Who must not fear to look upon the bride of Christ? But when a sermon is preached with the eyes and the face she looks at me, but not I at her." He often said that women were frivolous. "What business should a friar minor have to transact with a woman?" Yet, in contrast, one of his last acts was to write a letter to Giacoma di Settisole, a lady of Rome, asking her to hurry to his bedside if she wished to see him before he died. "Bring with you some of that ash-colored monastic cloth to wrap my body, and the wax needed for my burial," he requested. "And also I beg you to bring me some of that food you used to give me when I was sick in Rome."[6] These are hardly the remarks of a man who disliked the opposite sex.

When I read of these incidents I see a man who expressed detachment in the company of women, not one who disliked them. Obviously, he'd trained himself to remain reserved in their presence, aloof possibly, but never dismissive. At no time in his youth was he ever considered to be anything other than someone who enjoyed the company of young ladies. As master of the revels in his early years it was his responsibility to be sociable, anyway. What I do see at work here, however, is an ambivalence toward sexuality. In this respect, was Francis all that different to many of his time? Notwithstanding the troubadour influence, which mostly appealed to the taste of the aristocratic class, in general women were not considered to be much more than chattels in medieval society. They could be married off as pawns in the political game, they had few legal rights, and bearing children was

---

6. It appears that appetizing morsel was made from almond and honey cake.

their sole presumption over men. Clearly Francis was not all that out of kilter with prevailing opinion. Certainly his biographers felt no pangs of guilt about relating his attitude toward women—because they probably shared them also.

So I wasn't ready to believe that he disliked women. Nor was I prepared to accept that Francis rejected them because of some inherent defect.[7] It is simply that he knew his weaknesses, knew also that the path he had chosen required him to enact a particular kind of abstinence. He had to give up the fullness of being that the presence of a woman might offer him in return for something far more difficult to obtain. This was not to disparage women as beings, but as objects. He understood more than most the difference between the two, and how easy it was to succumb to the Eve in a woman, and so reveal the faltering Adam in himself.

In any event, Clare was so powerfully affected by his vision that she decided to abandon her life as the daughter of a noble, and take her chances as an ascetic. Living as we do in a secular age, it is hard to understand the motivations of a young woman from a deeply Christian family (her sister and her mother later followed her into the religious life) wanting to quit society and found an enclosed order of her own. It smacks of life-abandonment in the face of such tantalizing opportunities that must have existed for her in the enclosed environment of aristocratic privilege. Yet she was not afraid to do so, and this at the age of seventeen.

The final argument against any charge of misogyny being leveled at Francis pertains to Clare herself. If women were the enemy, then why did he give to her so much of himself? Why did

---

7. One only has to see the picture of Eve tempting Adam in the Brancacci Chapel in Florence, painted by Masaccio. Here, we see a voluptuous Eve grasping the Tree of Knowledge in the presence of Adam. Clearly, she is the Temptress. Though painted in the fifteenth century, it expresses ideas and attitudes about womanhood that reach back to Francis's day. It seems that man is the weaker sex when it comes to resisting the lure of the carnal.

he so influence her to give up normal life in favor of retiring from the world? I suspect it was because he recognized in Clare something unique: that she was, like few of us are, a true aristocrat of the spirit. Francis was in the business of gathering about him people worthy enough to be considered as members of his *illuminati*, male or female. To join such a fraternity, both sexes must remove themselves from the realm of the carnal. This was an obligation. He wanted people to recognize that sexuality is not evil but a hindrance to understanding, or experiencing, transcendent intuition. For him, sex was a corporeal emotion that must remain in the realm of the carnal. There it had its uses. But for a man, or woman, who wished to explore a deeper reality, one contingent upon knowing and understanding the role of Deity in their lives, then sex was, by its very nature, a hindrance. This isn't to disparage sexuality, but to recognize its limitations.

So the relationship between Francis and Clare cannot be assessed using the normal criteria of attraction. To do so would be to denigrate a relationship of extreme complexity—a relationship, in other words, that did not find its inspiration in the normal male-female interaction. Clare was not necessarily drawn to Francis by a powerful physical attraction, even if that were to be countenanced in the way we understand it today. And even if she had been, at no time could that expectation have been realized given their relative social standing. No, what transpired between these two young people partook of something altogether different: I believe they were inspired by a mutual desire to achieve a state of bliss. It was the idea of bliss that pressed them into a recognition in one another their heavenly counterpart.

This idea may not be so easy to understand or accept. In an age of emotional love, the concept of a spiritualized love sounds inconceivable. Such a love is the stuff of medieval romance, of *chanson de geste*. Can a twenty-nine-year-old and a seventeen-year-old suppress their natural instincts to the point where another sort of love might blossom? Judging by their portraits, both were attractive people in their own right; so what level of mutual resolve was brought to bear in favor of realizing a more elevated love? It is the question that none of the commentators have answered adequately in the past—I think because it requires a deeper knowledge and understanding of the nature of love than is normally experienced by monk or cleric, among the first people to write about Francis's life.

It occurred to me as I sat before the body of Clare that I was looking at—no, contemplating the remains of—someone whose relationship with Francis presaged that of Dante and Beatrice sixty-four years later. But with one difference. It is arguable whether Beatrice was ever conscious of her role as the supreme object of adoration for the poet. Whereas Clare knew that Francis had chosen her. She knew that he wanted her to make a particular kind of sacrifice in order to join him in a "marriage of the spirit." For her, this represented a unique opportunity. Francis's extraordinary powers of persuasion encouraged her to believe that she, too, may be capable of traveling her own path toward realizing a personal spiritual insight.

One must be aware of the poignancy of such a moment. Without knowing it, a young woman of seventeen finds herself making a decision that will eventually affect the course of Western spirituality. She decides to cross the boundary of social probity and commit herself to an unknown future as an ascetic in a "brotherhood" not yet countenanced by the Church. In medieval times such an act must have been regarded as one of absolute madness. Yet she did it. She fled her home in Assisi one dark night, and hurried into the somewhat amazed arms of the brothers living in their reed huts at Portiuncula. As a display of courage, surely it rivals that of Francis standing naked in the town square six years earlier.

She did this for love. It was love both for the man and what he represented. She saw in Francis what Dante perceived in Beatrice, and Ibn Arabi saw in Nizam, the daughter of a local sheikh in Mecca, because in the end both parties would have reciprocated this "glance." Allow Ibn Arabi to relate his experience:

> NOW THIS SHEIKH HAD A DAUGHTER, *a lithesome young girl who captivated the gaze of all those who knew her, whose mere presence was the ornament of our gatherings, and startled all those who contemplated it to the point of stupefaction. Her name was Nizam, and her surname "Eye of the Sun and of Beauty." Learned and pious, with an experience of spiritual and mystic life, she personified the venerable antiquity of the entire Holy Land. The magic of her glance, the grace of her conversation were such an enchantment that when, on occasion, she was prolix, her words flowed from the source; when she spoke concisely, she was a marvel of eloquence; when she expounded an argument she was clear and transparent....If not for the paltry souls who are ready for scandal and predisposed towards malice, I should commend her on the beauties of her body as well as her soul, which was a garden of generosity....*[8]

*

These remarks encapsulate the encounter I believe Francis and Clare experienced. The older man recognizes in the young woman qualities only visible to someone who was capable of perceiving them in the first place. He alerts her to their beauty and significance. He makes Clare conscious of the intensity of her nature toward the realization of something that went beyond herself. Moreover, in Clare he saw an emerging spiritual

---

8. Quoted from the Divan "The Interpreter of Ardent Desires" from *A Collection of Mystical Odes by Ibn Arabi,* translated by R. A. Nicholson.

genius like himself. In spite of her youth she was a woman blessed with the gift of seeing herself as a vessel for that deep interior recognition of God that lies in everyone. This was what she had seen in Francis; and this is what Francis had witnessed in her. Together, these two people made up a whole. Theirs was a true mystic marriage.

Clare's life was a testament to the transfiguring power of an idea—that of holy poverty and its ability to hone sensibility to the point where it could cut through the artifice of any false spirituality. She spent over forty years in the little monastery of San Damiano, practicing a particular kind of asceticism. It was said when she returned from her prayers that her face seemed more radiant and beautiful than the sun. Sometimes she lay for long moments on the ground of the oratory she had built in honor of the Holy Virgin. "When she returned from her prayer, the sisters rejoiced as if she had come from Heaven," said Sister Pacifica, an old family friend and fellow convert, in the canonization trial of Saint Clare. All her life, it seems, Clare remained true to the Rule that Francis had devised for her order. All her life she demonstrated a sweetness and simplicity that became an ornament to the memory of her greatest love. As Thomas of Celano later wrote, "she broke the alabaster of her body with discipline, so that the Church could be filled with the fragrance of her scent."

But I like to think that Clare wasn't so singularly motivated. In all the writings about her life, the woman emerges from the page as someone with a strong yet gentle will, a person not afraid to tackle the thorniest of issues, that of her profound and undiminished love for Francis. He, clearly, was her lodestone that she courageously sublimated into the love of Christ. Though he rarely visited her in her cloister during the active years of his ministry, I have the feeling that Clare was always on his mind, a memory, a savor, a taste of that mysterious moment when their lives, figuratively at least, became entwined. She, like him, remained true to their youthful vision. The shapeliness of the spirit made up for the lost physicality of his presence.

I cannot blame him for not visiting her more often. His was a difficult path to travel. After all, his vision had been founded upon the denial of the body. To be seen too often in the company of Clare would have placed this central tenet of his belief in jeopardy. Heloise experienced the same frustration as Clare, often complaining by letter to Abelard that he did not visit her enough in her convent. She too had become a nun, feeding off the memories of her once great love. Today we may see these acts of restraint as being somewhat extreme, wondering how any self-imposed absence might strengthen and deepen spiritual resolve. But that would be to miss the point. People like Abelard and Heloise, Clare and Francis, live by different rules than those given to any of us.

Gazing at Clare's body in its gilded cage, I was reminded of the fact that it was as recently as 1850 that her remains were discovered buried in the rock beneath the altar of the church. For six hundred years she had lain there, sleeping her long sleep, dreaming of the man who had inspired her to such a uniquely vigilant life in the service of her Lord. When they exhumed her she was not clutching a bunch of lilies as she does today. Rather, in her frail hands, so withered, so birdlike, there lay a copy of the monastic Rule that Francis had carefully prepared for the Poor Clares to live by. It seems that even in her last breath this remarkable woman had reached out for what had sustained her most: the knowledge that holy poverty, chastity, and obedience were the indices of a complete life.

CHAPTER SIX

The Sign of the Tau

✳

I t is interesting to see how we adopt symbols to give our life meaning, to root it in a more familiar soil. Secularism, for all its energy and sense of newness, is rarely able to invoke the timeless. Nonetheless, we submerge ourselves in it, hoping that it will soothe us and so make up for any loss of cultural memory. Yet in our hearts we know that it cannot act as a palliative. What we long for can only be summoned up by some powerful image, a sacred image, an image that stands above methodology or the voice of opinion. We look for signs in the landscape, observe certain forms and give them a name, cling to events that seem to have substance. In the end, we are thrown back upon that great quiver of symbols that our forefathers shot into the dark in order to make sense of existence.

I am talking about the way Francis endeavored to make a metaphor out of his own life. Unlike many saints of the past who relied on an almost sublime rectitude to hit the mark, one always feels that in his case a more subtle energy was at work. He wasn't just a good man, a man of noble works, someone who radiated humility. If the truth be known, he did very little that was practical except rebuild a couple of ruined churches. His gift rather was to inspire others, to give sermons, to indulge in prayer and meditation. His path was one of apophaticism: that is, to negate practical activity by way of poverty, obedience, and chastity in order to realize a deeper understanding of Divinity.

To this end, he was wary of learning. I think he saw intellectual knowledge as an impediment to what he felt was the primary object of the spiritual life—to attain to a simplicity of heart. When men of learning approached him to join the brotherhood, he always asked them to give up their calling as writers, thinkers, as intellectuals. He didn't want men who might challenge his Rule with the tools of dialectic. Nor did he want theologians in his midst, unless they were prepared to abandon disputation and humbly submit to the Rule.

One theologian did slip through the net, however: none other than Anthony of Padua. Born around 1195 in Lisbon, Anthony joined the Augustinians in Portugal, and later became a friar minor in Francis's brotherhood in 1220. But before that he studied theology, until he finally abandoned it at Francis's request. Yet, when the friars of Bologna asked that Anthony be released from his vow, Francis agreed. He sent him north with his blessing, knowing that the man would put his intellectual skills to good use as a teacher. He was named a Doctor of the Church in 1946.[1]

The simple fact was that Francis could be contradictory. Or more correctly, he addressed each case on its merits. He was no iconoclast eager to have done with the past. Far from it: no man clung more tightly to the apron strings of the Church than he. Nearly all his pronouncements were in support of canonical hierarchy and the authority of the pope. Thus, I found myself deal-

---

※ ————

1. There is a letter addressed to Anthony from Francis himself. It reads: "To Brother Anthony, my 'bishop,' Brother Francis sends greetings. It pleases me that you read [that is, teach] sacred theology to the friars, provided that amid such study you do not extinguish the spirit of prayer and devotion, as it is contained in the Rule." We hear a simple, clear voice at work, not one of an intellectual.

ing with a man whose revolutionary temperament was confined solely to the conduct of the individual. He saw human beings as the only fit tableaux upon which to exercise their spiritual artistry. For him, truth was the manifestation of error underpinning the idea of correctness, without which a certain kind of person could not live. He was just such a person. The "error" he wanted to alert the world to was the value of denial, asceticism, and the progressive diminution of the senses—all, I suppose, considered to be life-detracting under normal circumstances. Certainly, these values would not be considered by most as a way of approaching truth.

These ascetical practices were already familiar to the early Christian Church, having their origin in the anchorites of Egypt and a long history of monastic discipline in Europe. That Francis had chosen to return to the primitive Church for his inspiration, however, was an innovation. The Western Church had long ago abandoned the simple piety of the desert anchorites. It had become instead a monolithic structure firmly entrenched in the social fabric of its age. Francis's message was a restatement of a much older one: go back to basics. Spurn comfort, privilege, wealth, security, and public position, and begin to treat yourself and your very body as a chrism of truth.

To embrace this life of renunciation, and so to recommend it to others, Francis needed his own symbol through which he might act. He chose the ancient symbol of the tau, a device that was first used in Christianity by Saint Anthony, the original anchorite. Its origin was much older, of course. The Egyptian symbol of the ankh—meaning "life"—from which the tau is derived, was a popular image on the walls of Egyptian temples and on documents associated with the priests of Amun. That Francis should choose it above all others tells us a lot about where his sympathies lay. He wanted his ministry to be associated with a much older Christianity than the one that existed in his time. Did he, indeed, identify with Saint Anthony? It is hard to tell. But we do know that he often signed his letters with the sign of the tau, together with a tiny image of a skull.[2] It seems that life and death were made cohorts among his complicated canon of symbols.

It is a strange piece of heraldry, the tau. It has an archaic power about it, like a wooden mask outside a tribal hut in New Guinea. Unlike most other European heraldic devices it displays none of the sophistication or elegance that we expect to see on family coats-of-arms. Francis, a merchant's son, had deliberately chosen a device that reflected his outsidedness, his devotion to all things pertaining to the primitive. The tau was also known as the "Greek cross," again a reflection of Francis's desire to be associated with a more Eastern vision of Christ. It's no accident that all his life he had wanted to visit the Holy Land as a crusader. His face was firmly turned toward a simpler, more mystical vision of Christ's life and message. The harsh stones of Olivet were his pillow, not the comfortable featherbedding of his earlier life in Assisi.[3]

✳ ─────────

2. In a letter to Brother Leo, one of his closest friends, he drew these images. On the lower part of the parchment, Leo notes: "In like manner with his own hand he made this sign, the Thau, and the skull." The letter was written after he had been visited by the seraph at La Verna, and received the Stigmata. It is a simple blessing, laced with an enormous sense of absence, as if Francis knew that he wasn't long for the world:

May the Lord bless thee and keep thee;
May he show his face to thee and
*   have mercy on thee.*
May he turn his countenance to thee
*   and give thee peace*
The Lord Bless thee, Brother Leo.

✳ ─────────

3. There is a story told by Thomas of Celano of how Francis was attacked by a devil in his feather pillow one night. "It happened at the hermitage of Greccio, when he was suffering more than usual with the infirmity of his eyes, that he was forced against his will to use a pillow. On the first night, at an early hour, the saint called his companion and said to him: 'I have not been able to sleep tonight. My head shakes, my knees grow weak, and my whole body shakes as though I had eaten bread made from darnel. I believe,' he added, 'that the devil dwells in this pillow under my head.'"

I first encountered the tau in the monastery of Le Celle, in a valley outside the walls of Cortona. Francis founded Le Celle from a gift of land made by a wealthy citizen of Cortona in 1211. To-day, it consists of a group of close-packed buildings located on a steep hillside, above the banks of a torrent. Crossing a bridge be-tween vegetable gardens and fruit groves, I found myself outside a tiny doorway leading into Francis's cell. Inside the first room, now a chapel dedicated to his memory, one feels a strange air of solitude about the place. Sitting on a bench against the wall and gazing at the simple altar, I found myself meditating on this re-markable, if quixotic, man.

Francis, I told myself, you spent your life overturning con-ventional modes of belief and thought. It's not that you were highly literate, philosophically minded, or able to influence people through the brilliance of your argument. You wrote basic Latin and relied on a single-mindedness to make your point. Yet, in an equally strange way, you were able to influence kings, nobles, and popes. Was it simply charm? Did you exercise some native wit that has failed to translate down through the centuries? Or was it that something altogether special radiated from your person? Were you in possession of what holy men in Islam sometimes carry about their person, a quality known as *baraka,* that indefinable power of grace?

These questions were worth asking. I felt strongly that the sort of person Francis had been was of some importance in my attempt to understand where he was coming from. It was nearly eight hundred years since he had stepped inside this rock-hewn cave and laid down his head on an unfeathered pillow. It seemed like only yesterday, such was the strong sense of his presence still emanating from the roof beams and walls. I wanted to think that he was still very much with us, even though his bones lay in a crypt in the basilica of San Francesco in Assisi. I wanted to be-lieve also that his *baraka,* his spiritual radiance, hadn't yet been extinguished, in spite of tourism, trinket shops, and the hoards of cars and buses jamming roads in and out of Assisi.

I read somewhere that it is not enough to exercise imagination in these situations, but to *undergo* imagination. If I thought about that in relation to Francis, it made sense. It wasn't enough to have read his life story, to know the places he had visited and, in some vicarious way, to have felt his presence in different places around Italy. This was all very fine as an act of empathy. But it seemed to me that something more was demanded—that I needed to adopt a new mode of perception if I were to ever fully understand the man. The real question was: what constituted the architecture of his perception? Was there a new set of verbs in the treasury of silence that I had yet to act upon?

The first thing I thought I should do was try to analyze the man. Firstly, he loved poetry, travel, asceticism, the company of men, and contemplation. He enjoyed food provided it was not in excess, lonely places, old buildings that had fallen into ruin, conversation, meeting with men of high office, and getting his own way. He was by nature a wanderer. He dreamt of far places, particularly Spain, Morocco, and the Holy Land. The proselytizer in him wanted to visit these places and spread his message. He liked the idea of standing among the pillars of some ruined stoa and announcing his vision, just like an ancient philosopher in Athens. There was something of the pedant about him, too, the man who always thought he knew more than his brethren.

Secondly, he liked animals. He was comfortable in their presence. They liked him, too. There's one delightful story of how, when he was staying in Greccio, a rabbit was brought to him, still alive, after having been caught in a trap. Francis spoke to the rabbit as if it contained a person: "Brother rabbit, come to me. How did you allow yourself to be deceived like this?" The rabbit, set loose by the brother, immediately fled into the arms of Francis. There it cuddled up to him, while Francis caressed it. "But when it was placed on the ground several times, the rabbit returned each time to Francis." A fish caught in a net in the lake at Rieti refused to leave the side of the boat after Francis had placed it back in the water. These examples reveal an interesting side to Francis. It seems that nature inexplicably gravitated to him as if he retained some energy, not readily discernible, that could only be detected by animals.

Thirdly, he possessed an extreme sensitivity toward paranormal phenomena. He could foretell the future as he did at Damietta, when he informed the crusaders that they would lose the upcoming battle with Malik al-Kamil's forces. This they dutifully did. He displayed an inordinate trust in allowing major decisions to be made by forces he had no control over. Before embarking for the Holy Land, the ship's captain refused to take all his followers because of overcrowding. Francis asked a child on the dock to make the choice of the twelve to accompany him (note the high symbolism of the number: it corresponded to Christ's twelve disciples). On another occasion, in an unnamed hermitage, in order to find out what God wanted of him, he resorted to opening the Bible at random for guidance. Not once, but three times. And in each case the same page, the same text dealing with Christ's crucifixion, greeted him. He knew then what his destiny was to be: to undergo many trials and tribulations before he too entered "into the kingdom of God." It became clear to me that Francis rather enjoyed putting himself in the hands of what for many might be regarded as a chaotic situation. With the aid of some strange, primitive insight, he allowed himself to confront situations where fate might be forced to intervene. Some might see this as a demonstration of his stupidity, or his gullibility; others of his desire to remain in close contact with primeval forces. I suspect he would argue that his failures had some value, anyway, in that the betrayals and infidelities that had accompanied them might generate their own form of poetry.

In contrast, there is another side to the man. Whatever else might be said of him he does have more than one side to his personality. Even if we look at him as a youth and later as a young man we are confronted with a fun-loving, fairly easygoing sort of fellow. He got along with almost everyone, including those he spent time with in a Perugian prison. He liked to stroll about town with his friends, joining in the revels and pageants. From all reports, he had a close relationship with his mother. Reports suggest, too, that his relationship with his father was probably fairly normal until he had made his decision to break with the family. One assumes that he visited France with his father at one time or another, so they must have at least partly enjoyed each other's company.

But something deeply affecting happened to him along the way. We do not know when it occurred. I don't think he did, either. Given his penchant for symbolizing events, I think he would have made much of it in the process of creating his own myth. Let me say at the outset: I believe that Francis was conscious of making his own myth. Nor do I see this in a modern way of "believing his own publicity." No, Francis understood the nature of mythologizing, since he had lived in his own myth from an early age. His love of chivalry, his attraction to troubadour poetry, his desire to visit the Holy Land, and his instinct for martyrdom—all these things make it easy to understand why he chose a highly individual ascetical path. He didn't want to become just another monk, safe in his order, going through the motions of the spiritual life. He wanted, rather, to transform his life through an act of intuitive recognition of God. It is the key to his extraordinary personality.

The extreme behavior that characterized the other side of him masked his desperate search for an inner identity. He knew, as no one else did, that he needed to fracture reality if he was ever going to get anywhere. He needed to break down the schema-form-ing predilection of people in their bid to secure knowledge, and that included his own. To do so, he felt impelled to break with his former self and set up one that was diametrically opposed. He realized that he hadn't come into the world merely to leave it undisturbed. Rather, his task was to take control of any rage or disgust he might feel about the spiritual condition of his time, and induce others to share with him his dream of a better world. To do so, he needed to overcome *what was normal* in himself, and arraign before that citadel certain newly acquired virtues which would allow him to reach the very height of contemplation—a state Thomas of Celano referred to as being "out of mind for God."

I find this a fascinating concept: that Francis deliberately manufactured for himself a new character, and a new personality, in the wake of his moment of enlightenment. This may sound odd, or impossible, given our penchant for believing that we are born into ourselves like wheat in its husk. Yet, if I propose another allusion: a hermit crab casts off one shell and takes on another as soon as it feels constrained. It's likely that Francis cast off his former self and entered another when he realized that the old one no longer allowed him room for growth.

The post-Perugia-jail Francis was fundamentally a different person. He went in as an idealistic youth and came out a man who had experienced despair. He had mixed with men at their most basic, when all their defenses were down. Though he never gave up his fascination for war, I suspect that he must have learned a thing or two in there about the futility of internecine conflict. In addition, he had been subject to the humiliation of incarceration at a time when he most wanted to express himself. Disillusionment may well have been the gravest wound that he suffered during that war.

In the years following, Francis set about overturning nearly all his values. Instead of being a sensualist, he opted for asceticism. Instead of living in a well-to-do household, he preferred a reed hut out in the open. Instead of augmenting his wardrobe each year, he satisfied himself with a rough woolen tunic. Shoes he abandoned for bare feet. Sleeping in a bed he rejected for a mat on the hard floor. Rather than care for himself he looked after lepers. For friends he chose the company of social outcasts. His own family he denied, and money he rejected. Possessions became anathema to him, as if they were tainted with an incurable infection. The very concept of belonging in any one place was dismissed. From here on he would subject himself to every conceivable affliction, mental or otherwise. The man wanted to reduce himself to the barest necessity: that of a haunted figure of ridicule, a voice for the dispossessed, and a person in league with the disenfranchised.

He had become symbol-less. Nothing sustained him more than the illuminating fire of belief. He began to occupy a space in the lives of others that was in its own way, white hot. He had turned himself into a man in whom the impenetrable nature of sanctity had become, for the first time, almost palpable. It was this incandescence that fired others to follow in his footsteps. Here was a man whose whole being resonated with the orchestrations of another kind of music, a more intimate music, a music that evoked the suggestive magic of forgiveness and love. Francis had found only one thing left to believe in: God's mercy, and the possibility that his sinful nature would be looked upon with benevolence.

Strangely enough, as I sat in the tiny chapel dedicated to his memory, I felt that I understood Francis better. He was no longer the remote saint, gifted with beatitude, the reluctant symbol of a nation. Nor did I see him as some mean-spirited misogynist ranting against the opposite sex. These were the classic either/or images that are used to pigeonhole historical figures that do not surrender their hidden complexity easily. In an age where psychology has become the ready tool of self-analysis, a man like Francis defies such categorization. What I was confronting in the form of his memory had already slipped through the net of comparison. He was unlike any other saint in history: a mixture of mystic, ecstatic, nomad, and poet. Saint John of the Cross was a great poet but no wanderer; Saint Catherine of Siena an ecstatic but for some no mystic. Francis, on the other hand, combined so many lines of energy and inner experience that it is hard to pin him down. But we long to, nonetheless.

Finally I peered into the room at the rear of the chapel, approaching it by way of a small doorway to one side of the altar. Behind it was a cell carved out of the rock. A narrow ledge on the far wall constituted his bed. It was barely wide enough for a child to lie down on. A niche to one side housed a crucifix—a tau, to be more precise. This object was my first encounter with Francis's heraldic device. It lay propped in the niche, an archaic dolmen-like piece of carved wood, now shorn of any association with either tree or branch. I kept thinking of the half-submerged True Cross said to have been discovered in a cistern in Jerusalem by Saint Helena, the mother of the first Christian Emperor, Constantine, in the fourth century. Such a relic took on almost mystic powers that possessed both Christians and Muslims alike.[4]

I tried to put myself in Francis's position as he lay on the bench and gazed up at this most personal of icons. Nights of self-mortification and lack of sleep had accentuated his sensitivity. The back of his head might have been sore from laying it on the bare wood. Morning light may have crept through the entrance to the cave, slowly climbing the wall to his bed. Yet what he saw

✳ ───────────

4. The True Cross was captured by Saladin at the Battle of the Horns of Hattin (1187), and subsequently buried under the threshold of the Great Mosque in Damascus so that every pious Muslim might step on it on his way into prayer. Chrosroes, Heraclius, and finally Richard the Lionheart fought over it at different times throughout history.

before him in the niche had mysteriously begun to glow, a scaffold of pure light, an uncanny fluorescence. His weak eyes could make out a pale, incendiary device. The tau would have been his sole anchor, grounding him in unplumbable depths.

I kept thinking of certain remarks made by Brother Giles, one of Francis's closest friends, about the nature and rewards of meditation. They are interesting in that they are probably similar to those that Francis had made at moments of intimacy with his friend:

> HE IS A GOOD CONTEMPLATOR WHO, *if he were to have his hands and feet cut off and his eyes taken out and his nose, ears, and tongue cut off, would care for or desire to have no other members or anything else that can be thought of in the whole world besides what he has and feels, because of the greatness of the most sweet, ineffable, and unutterable odor, joy, and consolation that he experiences.*

*

Is this what Francis felt when he lay in his cell at Le Celle? It is a powerful and explicit statement of what can happen when one engages in a serious and prolonged act of meditation. Moreover, it probably takes a lifetime to begin to experience such ecstasy. Francis, it seems, was a master at entering such states, at least in his final years. He knew how to shut out the world and enter what one anonymous English mystic called the "Cloud of Unknowing." Though I had never entered it myself, I was conscious of how important it was to believe that such a state could be attained. Without the presence of the Unknowing, could our lives be anything more than a line dangled in some stream hoping for the occasional bite?

Le Celle was a turning point for me, as I suspect it must have been for Francis. It's not easy to come to terms with asceticism as a way of life, especially in our present age of affluence. But such relative affluence existed throughout history, and still human beings were drawn to a life of extreme restraint in their bid to counteract it. Why? What made them reject all that makes life comfortable? It's easy to argue that imbedded in Christianity is a collective masochism and self-loathing that encourages such practices. Yet this argument doesn't hold. I rather think that we miss the point if we make the contrast between the idea of comfort and the ascetical impulse in order to score a few points.

Asceticism is founded upon a desire to pacify the ego. It relies on a basic premise that the will must be released from its willing in order to rest within itself. It allows also for the realization of what Martin Heidegger called a "patient noble-mindedness." The benefits of such an engagement are intangible but real. All ascetical disciplines, from Mount Athos to Egypt, from India to Japan, acknowledge that meditation (prayer) unlocks the door to this singular room. But in order to enter the room one must have centered one's life in a particular way. It is at this point that asceticism begins to play a part. Ascetical practice composes the will and prepares the mind for its encounter with the "sweet fruits" of meditation.

Francis, I'm sure, knew what he was doing when he subjected Brother Donkey to the metaphoric whip. He recognized early in his life that his sensuous nature had made him too likable, too amenable to the desires and expectations of others. Being a son, a merchant, a master of revels, a husband, a father, a leading citizen, possibly even a crusader—all these personas were in the end inimical to achieving a concentrated life of patient noble-mindedness. Each one of these masks had to be given up if he were ever to realize his dream, the positioning of his life within the precinct of intuitive revelation. For that is what he wanted most: to become a vessel for humble patience and unique high-mindedness. He knew, as few of us will ever do, that a person discovers little, if anything, in the course of a life—but rather, is made use of in the realization of truth.

For Francis, the tau represented a return to a naive and undistorted vision. He wanted to reveal to people that in spite of the rapidly changing material circumstances of his time, the world would not necessarily be improved by either increasing affluence or social stability. Without a third leg on the stool, he knew it would fall over. His whole life became an enactment of this third leg. He wanted to show people by example that it was possible to engage in a life that drew its sustenance from beyond the horizon of human awareness. What lay beyond this horizon was not so easy to understand or to express; yet he felt that it was his duty to act at as a pathfinder. That his methods were neither original nor particularly informative at the theological level is immaterial. What he brought to the task was something unique. He showed the world that one could live a *poetic* life while embracing the spiritual.

The tau was his staff, his act of poetry. It bore his weight through Umbrian winters and the hot days of summer. It carried him up mountain paths to remote hermitages. It lay beside his bed as he attempted to ease the fatigue from his bones. It stood against the walls of the grottos into which he retreated in order to commune with his Maker. It cast a shadow on evenings as he made his way homewards to Portiuncula, or returned to the Christian camp at Damietta after talking with the sultan of Egypt. Wherever he went he leaned on this remarkable symbol of life and repentance. For he knew, as no one else knew, that the archaic image still has power to intensify his feeling for inner life.

CHAPTER SEVEN

Sister Swallow
& Co.

✳

In the tiny hill town of Alviano in Umbria there's a chapel in the castle dedicated to the occasion when Francis asked the swallows to be silent during his sermon on the steps below. An unknown painter has depicted a number of scenes from the saint's life, including a large fresco of this particular incident. It is a formal portrait of various people of the town gathered about the saint. Above, a group of swallows are in attendance. Though barely visible in the upper part of the picture, one senses that they are the real subject of the fresco. Thomas of Celano described the scene with all his concern for detail:

> WHEN ALL THE PEOPLE *had fallen silent and were standing reverently at attention, a flock of swallows, chattering and making a loud noise, were building nests in that same place. Since the blessed Francis could not be heard by the people over the chattering of the birds, he spoke to them, saying: "My sisters, swallows, it is now time for me to speak, for you have already spoken enough. Listen to the word of the Lord, be silent and quiet until the word of the Lord is finished."*

And those little birds, to the astonishment and wonder of the people standing by, immediately fell silent, and they did not move from that place until the sermon was finished.

✳

At the behest of Francis, nature fell silent. To us, the idea that nature could be addressed in this way seems strange, echoing perhaps the incantations and prayers of tribesmen in the forest addressing their gods. We who have learned to control nature, and so to pacify it, find it difficult to understand that men once viewed nature in a different way than ourselves. They lived within its caring arms and not upon its surface. Nature proved to be an intrinsic dimension to their existence, not some entity that could be manipulated for gain. For Francis to ask for its silence in the context of his sermon was to acknowledge this relationship: man did have the right to make certain demands upon it, provided these might be reciprocated.

That begs the question, of course: How did Francis acquire his ability to address bird and animals? There's no record of him having ever possessed this talent when he was younger. To all intents and purposes he had little to do even with livestock. So why did he then begin to enter the domain of creatures? It was an issue that interested me, if only because I had spent years in the Australian desert among Aborigines. There I had also encountered a reverence for nature in the form of cave paintings, corroborees (ritual dancing), and song. Tribal peoples also possess a unique relationship with nature. They appear to see it as one large, shimmering icon.

We are left with numerous stories demonstrating Francis's ability to cross the border between the realm of self-consciousness into that of an unusually intense state of natural empathy. Like the Aborigines, he regarded creatures, and indeed all natural phenomena, as a manifestation of what he called an "image of goodness." The poet in him saw nature as an artifact, and God as the supreme artist. He recognized in nature a pervasive symbolism that allowed hidden correspondences to be invoked, whereby an object in nature reflects a quality or value. As Thomas of Celano remarked, "he saw behind things pleasant to behold their life-giving reason and cause." This is none other than the doctrine of *correspondences* that a whole generation of poets in the nineteenth century made into their credo. Both Gerard de Nerval and Charles Baudelaire were avid exponents.

"In beautiful things he saw Beauty itself," Thomas went on. Francis was able to see the pattern in the natural world and follow in its footsteps. "He spared lights, lamps, and candles, not wishing to extinguish their brightness with his hand, for he regarded them as a symbol of Eternal Light." According to Thomas, he walked reverently on rocks, because of Him whom he saw as *the* Rock. He even forbade a brother to cut down a whole tree for wood, so that the tree might continue to grow. Such was his sensibility that he asked a gardener one day not to plough up the border around an unexcavated garden. In spring, he wanted to see the greenness of the grass contrast with a bed of flowers. Every moment of his life was in some way intensified by his feeling for nature. Even his sensory perception was enhanced by a garden of sweet-smelling herbs. Worms he set aside from the road so that they would not be stepped on. He ordered honey and red wine to be placed out of doors in winter so that the bees might survive.

Clearly, Francis was no ordinary country bumpkin. His sensibility towards nature was not inherent but rather, deliberately construed. Nor was he some sylph-like creature who preferred life in the forest to that of a more normal tenancy. While there are many stories outlining his retreat to wild places, it is always for a reason. He had business to do there. Communing with God was not an act of communing with nature; and he, of all men, recognized the difference. When he went into the forest, or retired to a cave to pray, it was with one object in mind—to bridge the gap between the here-and-now and the impalpable. The grotto was his time capsule: it drew him out of himself, away from the pre-occupations of timeliness, into a realm where all dimension became redundant.

Nature is the language of the Invisible. To understand it is to enter into a dialogue with God—or so Francis thought.[1] Largely unlettered except for a smattering of French and a rough knowledge of Latin, he relied on his intuition and hypersensitivity to help him resolve difficult issues. When administration problems arose in the brotherhood, he always found a way to disarm those who might wish to cause him trouble. He fought a running battle, for example, with certain reformers who wanted to soften his injunction against absolute poverty. By appealing to their better nature, he usually won any argument. People, particularly the educated, found it hard to resist the persuasive tone of his voice.

So free was his manner that a learned doctor confessed after hearing Francis speak that it was impossible to commit anything he said to memory. His eloquence was like quicksilver: easy to see and feel, but when you tried to contain it as a form, it immediately splintered into myriad slivers. He had learned, too, how to use the language of physical expression to convey what he meant. "He would suggest in a few words what was beyond expression," Thomas wrote, "and using fervent gestures and nods, he would transport his hearer wholly to heavenly things." It becomes apparent that Francis liked to become *animated.* Was this the secret to his close understanding of nature?

His power of proclamation extended to the use of others as intermediaries. On one occasion, the city of Arezzo was riven by a civil war that threatened to destroy the place. Francis happened

---

1. For the medievals, the Word of God was the cosmos—the all-encompassing order, opposite of primeval chaos. Nature was the mediator of His operations.

to be in the vicinity, and he became aware of tremendous negative forces plaguing its inhabitants. He could feel them; evil was in the air. Rather than draw back and proceed elsewhere, Francis asked one of his friends, Silvester, to stand before the gate of Arezzo and demand that these devils quit the place. Within days, the city returned to normal. Whenever he later preached in the square, Francis always referred to the incident and the good fortune the inhabitants had experienced because of the prayers of a "certain poor man." Silvester had become the mouthpiece for an inordinate psychic energy, and Francis's willingness to express it through his friend. Visions and prophecies were a part of his stock in trade.

I mention Francis's gift of prophecy and his empathy with nature in the same breath, as I feel they are contingent. He had learned to see beyond the horizon of representation, and so was able to bring to bear an unusual kind of perception. What he saw, and how he saw it were different to the way we acknowledge things. The world of representation—that is, the world of objects in the factual sense—meant less to him than the world contained by mystery. Mystery is, as one writer observed, the realm that lies beyond the horizon, yet at the same time offers us its transcendent face. While we can occasionally view this face, we are at a loss to see behind it. Certain realities reveal themselves only to those who are equipped with what we loosely call a "sixth sense," which is something more subtle.

Francis derived his phenomenal intuitional sense from his understanding of the workings of nature. But his understanding was not a product of shallow observation, or the objective stance of the scientist. Nature literally spoke to him in the silent language of itself. Through meditation, prayer, and long bouts of asceticism, he had learned how to listen to the voice of nature. Most ascetics are equipped with this supernatural perception. There is a long history of mystics and anchorites engaging in dialogue with the creatures of the world. Ravens fed Saint Anthony in the desert; a lion from whose paw he had removed a thorn protected Saint Jerome. Daniel had no problem cohabiting with lions in their den. We know that Francis spoke to a wolf near Gubbio, and told the animal to mend its ways. Even in our own day, there are those who speak to horses, and so break them to saddle. All these have one thing in common: they are able to commune by way of an intuitional sense that enables them to bond with animals.

One must remember that animals in Francis's day were still very much in contact with wild space. That a man-eating wolf could roam the outskirts of a town like Gubbio is inconceivable today. That birds could dominate a conversation in a town square sounds ridiculous, given our penchant for electronic noise. Rabbits no longer wander the forest of Italy but are rather bred in hutches on backyard allotments. Hunting in Francis's day was an occupation—men roamed the countryside snaring pheasant, rabbits, and turtledoves for the market. Today, in our agribusiness environment, such wildness is remote, even to the animals. Animal flesh is now the stuff of the futures markets and the bottom line of corporations.

There is one story telling of how a young trapper snared some turtledoves near Siena. He was taking them to market along the road when Francis happened to pass. Francis persuaded the boy to part with the doves on the grounds that these birds were, in Scripture at least, the symbols of "pure, humble, and faithful souls." Francis took the birds in the folds of his tunic, and carried them home to the hermitage where he was staying. There he built a nest for them so that they might lay their eggs. In time, they bred. But they refused to leave the hermitage until Francis had given them permission. So impressed was the boy in this story when he heard of Francis' actions, that he later became a member of the brotherhood.

Francis utilized a falcon as a timepiece at one hermitage where he stayed. Retreating as was his wont to a cave to contemplate, the falcon, which had its nest nearby, used to announce with its song the hour when Francis was accustomed to rise for worship. The falcon acted as his goad, and "any delay on his part because of laziness was driven away." At that time, too, his eyes began to trouble him more than usual. The falcon took note of the situation, and refrained from announcing the time of the watches except at dawn, in order to give Francis time to rest.

How is this possible, one might ask? Pheasants, swallows, turtledoves, falcons, rabbits, and wolves—a whole menagerie was at his beck and call. The man seemed not to discriminate between human beings and animals. His conversations with animals, however, were always laced with the understanding that creatures were in some way a symbol of divine law. He knew that animals and birds, far from being the product of some Darwinian logic, carried the burden of Creation upon their shoulders. Like angels, they possessed no reflective power save that of pure being. This gave them their resilience, and their beauty, in their ability to reflect the slow evolution of human consciousness. In the way we handle animals so do we handle ourselves, he seemed to be saying. When we are cruel, when we manipulate their breeding and destroy their habitat, then do we devalue ourselves.

Francis was no idle dreamer when it came to his relationship with animals. Of course, the progressive urbanization of medieval society produced its own calculative hardness. People such as his father (and later the Medicis) could see profit in banking, manufacture, and distribution. It's no accident that at about this time banks came into existence (in Siena first), precipitating the slow accumulation of capital to which we are heirs today. Before this time, wealth creation had been a haphazard affair, the product of excessive taxation of the lower classes by noble families, and the movement of goods along the sprawling trade routes of the eastern Levant, which in turn resulted in a small but significant shift away from crop production and animal husbandry. It's no accident that this period corresponds with the rise of such trading states as Venice, Genoa, Pisa, and Florence. These city-states looked to the sea for their wealth, not to the land about them.

In early medieval art, too, we see a change in the role of animals as decorative motifs. They appear in more domesticated situations, and no longer act as motifs for space and wildness that they once did in Romanic art or the mosaics of Saint Apollinare in Classe in Ravenna. Until this point, animals still held their own against the progressive urbanization of the environment. The only exception to this is in the art depicting the circus, where wild animals were pitted against themselves, and occasionally against men. Yet, even in such cases, the animal is still seen as a contrast to people, a wild thing in possession of its own raw integrity. But when the domestic interior became the setting for art, so did the animal find itself reduced to a cipher for domesticity. The rise of the "purebred," be it horse or dog, echoes a desire to manipulate animals to reflect human consciousness. Now the animal has entered into a diminutive relationship with people. It has lost its separate entity in conjunction with nature. It had become little more than an appendage to mercantilism and its need for self-flattery.

Francis's attitude toward animals strikes us as being wholly against the instincts of his time. People were content to see livestock and the animals of the forest as economic integers only, not as reflections of God. Francis's primitive nature must have struck an odd chord among many who witnessed his acts of kindness. Even if they weren't aware of it, he was alerting them to another kind of relationship beyond that of mere utilitarianism. He was asking them to engage in the age-old art of correspondence, whereby "something other" might be evoked rather than organic recognition or the prospect of exploitation. Such an art went as far back as Aesop and his fables, which were first compiled by the Romans. Francis was merely reiterating a belief widely held in antiquity: that animals were the mirrors of nature.

At this point, one begins to see a pattern to Francis's thinking and behavior. With only a cursory acceptance of his dealings with birds and animals, one could be forgiven for believing him to have been little more than a harmless eccentric. The chroniclers' insistence that he spoke with them, and that he entered into their lives in some way, may even be seen as an example of naive enthusiasm for wonders and miracles. It's easy for us to argue that things didn't happen as they were recorded—that men wanted to believe in Francis's ability to transcend normal acts of communication and so embroidered his actions to support his claim to sanctity. Such is the action of an empirical mind, surely a blight upon a deeper understanding of his motives. If we accept that a mystery is the revealing of one aspect of the invisible through the medium of another, then it may be that Francis had devised a successful method of doing so.

I cannot claim to have any answers to these perplexing questions. But one thing I do know for certain is that Francis's penchant for reversing values has a good deal to do with it. Like all visionaries it's not so much how original he might have been, but how he found new and striking ways to express his vision. If "fervent gestures and nods" possessed sufficient power to change people's lives, then whatever constituted his magnetism—could not this also work on creatures? The mere fact that he proposed another reality to an age bent upon securing a place in the realm of materiality and calculative living; does this not suggest that he understood the dilemma confronting so many?

The truth is that medieval society was slowly destroying its relationship with wonder and the givenness of things. The mapmakers, the merchants, the sailors, the bankers, and the boat builders—all of them were setting humanity on a course toward the "world out there." While on the other hand Francis wanted to reaffirm the importance of the world within, a world that had always been acknowledged for its life-enhancing properties. He could see, as few could, that importing cloth from Flanders might well increase his father's material well being. He could also see that the accumulation of gold as a result of such trade had led to a decline in his father's spirit. Francis was fully aware that increased economic activity might improve the lives of many, but at a cost: the alienation of those who invested much of their being in the celebration of the Divine.

This, I think, lies at the heart of his dealings with nature. He proposed a love of it as an alternative to the desperate eagerness of those who wanted to replace it with an edifice of wiles. Medieval society was moving forward; it was shaking off the sleep of past centuries dominated by Latin copyists and the emerging power of the Church. While Francis would always accede to the Church in Rome, he was quick to abandon the hairsplitting habits of the theologians. Nature became his gospel because in it he could see with uncommon clarity the essence of his vision. It was to re-assert man's temporality in the wake of the illusory belief in a manufactured eternity.

His relationship with nature was an essential part of his aesthetic. Not since the late Roman poets had anyone thought to engage in a dialogue with it. The Christian Church had cloaked so much of the external world in dogma that it was hard to see the wood for the trees. Christ's suffering, particularly in the early medieval period, had overtaken Christ as the divine shepherd of human beings. Not until the sixth century was Christ ever portrayed on the cross. Until then, he was always seen as a more benign figure, a shepherd with the Lamb of God about his shoulders as we see him in Saint Apollinare in Classe. At this point, Christ was still portrayed as part of nature itself.

It was the image that Francis liked to carry about with him.

He wanted to see himself as a man for all seasons, and for all creatures. One might view his attitude as arrogant, the product of an overweening regard for his own powers. Not only human beings but also animals were at his beck and call. Was it not a form of hubris? I like to think not. I would rather believe that he understood better than any of us how important it is to acknowledge ourselves as part of nature. In an age such as our own, when nature has been stripped of its seasonal riches in order to fuel our appetites, the idea that a person might ask permission to partake of its bounty gives us food for thought. It may be that true spirituality is contiguous with a respect for and love of nature, that in destroying nature we are doing irreparable damage to ourselves.

I will always retain this image of Francis. He was a guardian of nature's inner resources. He understood something that we have forgotten: that nature conducts a symphony of its own so that all might enjoy it. When the nexus between it and us is broken, then the music of renewal will be lost forever. We will walk this earth, alone and unbidden, because neither swallow nor falcon will be there to announce that moment of prayer with their song. We would have lost the gift of meditation, and so condemned ourselves to existing in a state of uprootedness until the end of time. Francis, on the other hand, will always be with us as a memory of what we might have embraced before we chose to settle for a life of mere contrivance.

Alviano's frescoes are our visual memory of a remarkable event. When swallows fall silent in the wake of a sermon, then we can be sure that nature concurred with what Francis was saying. Standing in that chapel and gazing up at the faces of those in his audience, I somehow felt that I, too, was in that square on that historic day. What he spoke about is now forgotten; but the wild enthusiasm of a flock of birds suddenly falling silent to listen to his words is an image we will never forget. Nature, even today, wishes to impose its presence upon the more episcopal outbursts of men. It wants to be heard, if only at that moment when we ask it to tone down its enthusiasm for spring. But that doesn't mean that it has lost its voice.

CHAPTER EIGHT

In the Sultan's Domain

✳

I t's one thing to preach love and forgiveness in your own backyard, but to travel to foreign lands in order to announce your
message suggests some strange fascination with the other.
Francis was a man obsessed with distance. For all his restraint
and desire to live the simple life, there was a part of his character
that delighted in traveling beyond the bounds of what was familiar. Some might argue that his taste for travel might have been
inspired by his childhood memories of his father's journeys to
France. It may be true. He may have actually enjoyed being absent from home for long periods. He may even have enjoyed way-
side inns, dockyards filled with the sound of foreign tongues, and
the savor of simple food in lonely caravansaries.

I've tried to put myself in his shoes. His quixotic intellect made
him substantially different in outlook to his countrypeople.
Umbria was their much-loved land, of course—a land historically settled and ordered. The blood of Etruscans still coursed in
their veins. They were in no way Roman in outlook, preferring
the rich tapestry of decoration in their lives to the more prosaic,
unimaginative stance of those ancient invaders from the south.

It's no accident that Renaissance art found its most fruitful encounter with landscape in Umbria's forested valleys and lakeside towns. Who has not looked into the backgrounds of a Pintoricchio or a Lorenzetti and wondered about the actual location of their mysteriously painted townships? Are they cities of the mind? Or are they perhaps carefully rendered details drawn from Passignano, Castel del Lago, Spello, Trevi, Spoleto, or the high hill town of Panicale overlooking Lake Trasimeno?

Whenever I traveled about Umbria, I was always conscious of journeying through an imaginative landscape. All the hopes and fears of its people throughout the centuries were still very much imbedded in its stones. It was as if they had rendered into every wall and buttress a careful dream of the past married to an uncertain future. No wonder the bulwarks around villages were so thick, the watchtowers so high, the castles so austere and remote. I was traveling through a land that had long ago learned how to deal with the provisional nature of existence. It tended to freeze its image on brightly painted, kiln-fired pottery, in elaborate escutcheons carved on palace walls, in vast frescoes celebrating auspicious moments in local history, in gilded coats-of-arms painted on the ceiling of medieval council rooms, in heraldic pennants and elegant costumes that can still be seen today during festivals.

These images would have been familiar to Francis. He would have moved within this finely crafted world with a measure of indifference. But, nonetheless, it would have conditioned his perceptions, and made him the aesthete that he was. His was an educated eye, for he understood beauty as something bred into his bones. At no point in his career as an ascetic did he ever deny the wonder of his senses. He knew *how* to see things, to hear sounds, to engage in real acts of appreciation of the countryside he was walking through. It's no accident that all the monasteries he founded are located in remarkably beautiful spots. Whether clinging to a cliff-face like Greccio, or nestled among trees on a hilltop above Rieti like Fonte Colombo, or gracing a mountain valley as a terraced garden of buildings at Le Celle near Cortona, there was always one overriding consideration at work: that Francis understood, as few before him, how to transform wild terrain into a genuinely meditative space. His retreats are the retreats of a mind that understood how to integrate interiority and earth.

So why did he like to get away from Umbria? Why did he want to travel to Spain, to Morocco, through the Marche of Italy, to Ancona, and finally to Rhodes, Cyprus, Acre in the Holy Land, and to Egypt itself?[1] It's assumed that the missionary in him was bent upon proselytization and conversion, that he wasn't satisfied with local fame as a preacher and wanted to test himself on a foreign audience. It may be true: there's no denying that his belief in the superiority of Christianity over Islam inspired some of his more remarkable journeys. But I suspect there was more to it than simple missionary zeal. For one thing, Christians had long been dealing with Muslim peoples on an equal basis. They might not have liked them, but at least they recognized their high level of culture and civilization.[2] Even the crusading movement was not aimed at conversion; but rather, to reclaim the holy places in the name of Christianity. These wars were acts of colonization

---

* ————

1. Francis attempted to reach Morocco by way of Spain in 1213. Ostensibly, he wanted to convert its sultan, Moramolin. They say martyrdom was on his mind. There is some suggestion that he may have reached Santiago de Compostella on this journey.

* ————

2. I am reminded of how Frederick II, not long after Francis's death, sent out a questionnaire to Mohammedan philosophers all over the Middle East, inquiring into such issues as the eternity of matter, the immortality of the soul, and the number and nature of categories—surely proof that there was an active and respectful dialogue going on between Europe and the East. Arab philosophers were present at the Court of Roger in Palermo as early as the 1140s. Nearer to home, we find that the mathematician Leonard of Pisa received his education in North Africa, then in the Islamic domain.

waged under the cloak of Catholic missionary zeal. No one was under any illusion that the Holy Land represented anything other than a prime piece of real estate ripe for the taking by land-hungry European nobles.

Francis's desire to convert the heretics (Islam was seen by some theologians as no more than a Christian heresy) may have been the explanation given for his journeys, but I am beginning to wonder whether it was his real reason for making them. I suspect his chivalrous nature rather enjoyed the idea of making a trip to far places in search of the exotic. Moreover, he wanted to test his mettle against the spirit of the other. The secret mystic in him longed to engage in a dialogue with those who did not require an intermediary between themselves and God. Though Christ was his Savior, he still felt a hankering for the experience of the Absolute as a negation, divine and unadorned. My own opinion is that Francis vacillated between a strong belief in God as the Almighty reflected in the reality of Christ, and a mystic's image of God as some incomparable statement about a supreme and unknowable Nothingness.

I don't know why I say this, except that for a long time I have felt that his biographers never really understood the predicament he found himself in. They wanted to paint him as a simple saint, a pious ascetic whose commitment to poverty, chastity, and obedience satisfied the expectations they had of their own religious beliefs. It may be, too, that Francis's careful avoidance of all learning was his way of dealing with what he instinctively felt to be an ossification of theology over the past thousand years, and the dogma it espoused. The doctrine of the Trinity and differences with the Eastern Church over words in the Creed were issues that merely clouded what he believed to be Christ's role as a mirror of the Divine. He was trying to establish a new way of approaching the mysteries, of freeing them from the hegemony of doctrinal knowledge imposed upon them by theologians.

Too much dialectic had come between human beings and their understanding of God. Francis, who was reasonably well educated for his time, wanted to distance himself from doctrinal matters in the interest of evoking a new spiritual sensibility. He knew his Bible well, and his writings are littered with sayings that he'd cribbed from his reading. He had no qualms in plagiarizing the gospels if he thought it might contribute to his argument. So it can't be said that Francis avoided learning in the broad sense. It's just that he wanted it to be applied directly to the task of personal renewal, and not to the fabrication of any new theological doctrine. Without ever openly stating his case to the contrary, Francis was one of the earliest spirituals to distance himself from the Scholastics who were already beginning to dominate the debate about how and what people should believe.

I'm beginning to think that Francis led a clandestine life intellectually. He was an extremely good administrator in his early years, and wrote some incisive letters and homilies to the faithful on how they might led their lives in accordance with God's law. His Rule of 1221, written five years before his death, and likely to have been derived from an earlier more basic rule, is a masterpiece of spiritual and administrative good sense. To have written it would have required consummate knowledge of the spiritual life, as well as a strong understanding of how communal lives ought to be conducted. He also advised Clare on how to formulate her own rule in one of his letters. It is clear that Francis was no spiritual recluse, out of touch with the needs of his followers. At every stage of his ministry, he used his knowledge and his learning to influence the course of events.

All this is by way of exploring his reasons for journeying to the Holy Land and to Egypt. At one level, it was a perfectly normal aspiration for any Christian believer. Countless thousands made the pilgrimage to the holy sights in Palestine each year. The ports of Italy were flooded with people wanting to book passage to Acre, and many a ship owner made his living plying the Levant with a boatload of pilgrims. It's rumored also that Pica, his mother, managed to extract sufficient funds from Pietro for her own voyage to the Holy Land. Did Francis ever talk to her about her trip? Did she encourage him with stories of the marvels that she had witnessed? The chronicles are silent on the matter, as they are on any relationship between Francis and his parents after his conversion. It may well have been to reinforce the myth that he had utterly broken with his family in the interest of becoming a full-time ascetic.

I'm inclined to think that Francis's voyage to the Holy Land was unexceptional in this regard. If his mother could do it, then there's no reason why he couldn't. There is no actual record of what he did along the way, but we may assume that the trip took a minimum of three weeks in a fair wind. He probably slept on deck for the most part, and ate a simple meal with other pilgrims. We do know that his ship had a full complement of passengers, along with his dozen brethren. The very fact that he traveled with so many suggests that he wanted to leave some of the brothers in Palestine to bolster the tiny community already set up there. He was a man on a mission, not solely to convert the heathen but to strengthen the growing Europeanization of his order there. Palestine was fertile ground to plant yet more seed.

When he arrived, he probably visited many of the holy sites associated with Christ's life and death, if not earlier then probably later in his travels. There's no record actually stating that he visited Jerusalem. But if he didn't, his trip would surely have been a waste of a unique opportunity. He certainly didn't visit Palestine in order to venture forth to Egypt. This choice would have been a decision that he made once he was there, not before. For a man who had modeled his life on that of Christ's, I can only assume that he was more interested in visiting Jerusalem, the Holy

Sepulcher, Golgotha, Gethsemane, and Bethlehem in order to draw inspiration from the events in Jesus' life.[3]

One must not underestimate the power of Christ's story on men and women in Francis's time. The spirit of pilgrimage was as popular in his day as the Hadj is for Muslims in our own. It offered people the opportunity to escape the drudgery of medieval life in favor of visiting new lands, making new friends, while enjoying an experience that was fully condoned by the Church. We have few if any personal records of day-to-day life on the road to Jerusalem (carrying pen, inks, and parchment might have only added to the burden), but we must assume that there was a good deal of camaraderie experienced. Arriving in foreign ports would have been no less exciting than it is today. And the pilgrim would have had an added bonus for his pains: the prospect of visiting the places of the historical Christ, and so participating in the mystery of his origin.

When Francis arrived in Acre, it was to discover that the crusaders were besieging the Egyptian city of Damietta, in the Nile delta region. It was part of a strategy to cut off the supply of grain to the Muslims in Palestine, and so render them amenable to striking a deal over Jerusalem, which was still in Arab hands. Once more, the lure of a martyr's death reared its head: Francis wasted little time in taking ship to Egypt to be on hand when Damietta fell. What confronted him when he arrived was a soldiery that had long since abandoned the ideal of crusading. Discipline and morale were poor, camp followers were in abundance, and the papal legate, Cardinal Pelagius, hawkish by nature, was urging King John of Jerusalem (in exile, of course) to attack at once.

---

3. According to Angelo Coreno, Francis did visit the Holy Places under a safe conduct granted to him by al-Kamil's brother, the Sultan of Damascus. One can only assume that Francis was profoundly affected by his experience walking in the footsteps of Christ, his erstwhile hero. But he never reported on it.

The leader of the Egyptian forces was a man named Sultan Malik al-Kamil. The picture we gain of him is someone of a refined nature who enjoyed poetry, and who liked nothing better than to discuss religious issues. We know, for example, that the sultan enjoyed a correspondence with European princes such as Frederick II, who asked him to send to the Sicilian court someone well versed in astronomy, which he promptly did. He was deeply interested in Sufi mysticism, too, in particular the works of the Arab mystical teacher Umar ibn al-Farid. One of the central tenets of al-Farid's thought was the idea of effecting an intense love for an intensely personal God. As it happens, this idea was not all that dissimilar to that held by Francis. The sultan viewed the forthcoming battle with the crusaders as a disaster for the entire economy of Egypt, which relied heavily on a large European contingent of merchants and traders living in Alexandria and the delta region. The loss of the city would have crippled such trade.

It was this man that Francis conceived a desire to meet. After one battle between the two armies on August 29, 1217, which he had foreseen as a disaster for the crusaders, Francis found himself to be not all that popular among the Christian leaders after their debacle. More than four thousand men were killed, yet still al-Kamil held back from storming the crusader encampment. Instead, he offered the Christians a truce that they accepted. It was during the lull in military activity that Francis decided to cross over into enemy lines in an attempt to seek an audience with the sultan. Was it to work out a peace agreement as Cardinal Pelagius encouraged, or was it to debate theology with the Muslim sages as the chronicles relate?

It couldn't have been an easy task to make it through the lines. He was variously roughed up by guards, threatened with beheading, and finally put in chains before being led before the sultan. Possibly because he came escorted only by Brother Illuminato that the guards believed him when he demanded to see the sultan. His request was so absurd that they felt he must have something important to say that might lead to a victory over the accursed infidels. We can visualize Francis, accompanied by Brother Illuminato, the sole eyewitness of ensuing events, walking through the gates into Damietta, dragging their chains. At the height of the siege, let us hear how Jacques de Vitry, then the bishop of Acre, related what he believed to have occurred in his *Eastern Chronicles*:

> NOT ONLY CHRIST'S FAITHFUL, *but also the Saracens and their allies admire the humility and perfection of these people [the Franciscans]. For they go to them, and they, being granted the right spirit, receive them happily. We have seen the first founding master of their order, a simple and unlettered man, delightful to God and men, named Brother Francis: he was so inspired with exhilaration for heavenly things, and so caught up in the spirit of service, that when he came down to the Christian army at Damietta in Egypt, with a single companion he went fearlessly, armed with the shield of faith, to the Sultan of Egypt. And when they were in the Saracen lines he said: "I am a Christian. Take me to your master." And when they dragged him before him, the cruel beast seeing him, in aspect so much a man of God, gentle in manner, he listened to him, and his people, most attentively over a period of days, preaching the faith of Christ. But at length, seeing that none from that army was actually converted to God, they crossed back to the Christian lines, being led back into our camp with all reverence and safety.*

✳

If only Jacques de Vitry had realized how incongruous this reads. On the one hand we hear of Francis being granted audience by a "cruel beast," yet on the other we hear how he listened "attentively over a period of days" to reasonable arguments put forward by reasonable men. One gains a strong suspicion that Francis's sojourn was written about with propaganda in mind. Nor would have Francis wished to invite criticism by disclosing details of his discussions with the sages and poets at the sultan's court. It may be, as Idries Shah suggests, that Francis wished to question Sufi teachers there about their special methodology known as *dhikr,* the ritual act of remembering, so similar to the technique of "holy prayer" developed by Francis himself. It may be no accident either that the Franciscan dress, with its hooded dress and wide sleeves, is the same as that of the dervishes of Morocco and Spain.

There are other similarities between Sufis and the way Francis conducted his spiritual life. We note that he never became a priest, and sought to spread his message among all the people. This is how Sufis operate, even today. We know that he saw a seraph with six wings at La Verna, an allegory also used by Sufis to convey the formula of the *bishmillah.* It was Francis's salutation as well: "The peace of God be with you!" He was reputed to have thrown away spiked crosses that were worn for the purpose of self-mortification by many of his monks. Such an action may or may not have been reported exactly. Rather, it may resemble the Sufi practice of ceremonially rejecting a cross with the words, "You may have the cross, but we have the meaning of the cross."[4] One final similarity between the Sufis and Francis was in his rejection of personal salvation as the primary object of asceticism. He, like the

---

4. This practice could be the origin of the Templar habit, alleged by witnesses, suggesting that the Knights "trod on the cross" as part of their rituals. It was used later as evidence in their trial inferring that the Templars blasphemed the cross.

Sufis, may have regarded salvation as an expression of vanity, since it placed too much emphasis upon one's personal spiritual expectation.

I have already alluded to the interpenetration of ideas between Islam and the West. Men such as Roger Bacon, Raymond Lull, and Albertus Magnus, the teacher of Saint Thomas Aquinas, openly acknowledged their debt to Islamic thought. Pope Silvester was reputedly a magician who had graduated from Arab schools. Duns Scotus and Saint John of the Cross were also deeply influenced by the Illuminist school of thought founded by ibn Massarah of Cordoba in the ninth century. Dante's entire cosmology owes a great deal to another great Illuminist, Suhrawardi, who was put to death in Aleppo in 1191 on the orders of Saladin, shortly after Francis was born. Indeed, his Mystic Rose is a variation on the Sufi phrase "path of the rose." There is some evidence to suggest that Massarah's work inspired a Jewish thinker from Malaga, Solomon ibn Gabirol, whose work in turn influenced the Franciscan school. It may be inferred that there was an invisible network of Illuminist thinkers stretching from Spain to the Middle East. They slowly spread through Italy by way of Palermo where a group of translators were at work at the Court of Roger, and later Frederick II. It seems that men like Francis and his friends may not have been immune from certain aspects of Sufi thought in whatever disguise it reached them—even those imbedded in Cathar beliefs.

So the discussions Francis conducted with the learned at the sultan's court no longer sound like the work of a fanatic and proselytizer. Of course, arguments about one religion or another would have arisen, but more likely in the spirit of open inquiry than that of denigration. I cannot see the court sages granting Francis so much of their time if they felt that they were dealing with a man unsympathetic to their ideas. Not having to deal with the constraints of doctrine as he might have back in Italy, I suspect

Francis rather enjoyed the opportunity to explore the subtleties of theology with his hosts. They, in turn, while recognizing his unique personality, must have found the encounter equally enlightening. Any suggestion that he might have challenged his hosts to an ordeal by fire to prove the superiority of Christianity sounds like the argument of apologists desperately trying to justify his visit in the first place. Neither Thomas of Celano nor Saint Bonaventure, two of his earliest biographers, mention that such an event took place. Though I note that Giotto painted the scene in one of his magnificent frescoes in the basilica of San Francesco, so the event did hold popular appeal.

Francis witnessed the final destruction of Damietta by the crusaders when it was taken without a fight, due to illness and starvation. What happened next must have tried his humanity: one in ten of the 3,000 inhabitants were kept as hostages, the rest were either butchered, sold into slavery, or given to the Church as bondsmen. The nearby city of Tanis was sacked shortly after, and little mercy was shown to its inhabitants. What Francis saw there left him disillusioned. He "saw sin and wickedness among the soldiers, and was troubled by it. For that reason he left." Clearly he had met with a better reception from the sultan than from his own kind.

What memories did Francis retain of his trip to the Holy Land? The chronicles are silent on the matter. Knowing how sensitive he was to place, however, I cannot believe that he did not react positively to his encounters with the holy sites around Jerusalem. To visit the Holy Sepulcher was the supreme experience that the medieval world offered the Christian pilgrim; and Francis would have sensed this as he tramped along the Via Dolorosa or stood in the incense-filled churches of the city, gazing at their icons. It was the moment he had wished for all his life—to participate in Christ's agony, and to know that it was not in vain. He, the poor man of Assisi, had made his own sacrifice.

In the basilica of San Francesco there's a small museum dedicated to articles said to have belonged to Francis. I discovered a small reliquary enclosing a piece of cloth bearing a hole said to have been made by the Stigmata in his chest. The letter to Brother Leo signed with the tau is here, too. Even his habit, a worn, much-patched piece of cloth, is laid out fanlike beneath glass. The repair work is delicately rendered; suggesting that whoever did it (Francis himself, perhaps?) knew how to sew. But what really caught my attention was a finely decorated horn made from ivory, attached to a set of rings by small chains. The rings were also chained to two small whip handles that, according to the legend, were a flagellation tool (*"corno e bastoncini d'avoro"*). These were a gift of Sultan al-Kamil.

Suddenly I was back in Damietta, sitting about on a divan listening to Francis talking with the Muslim and Coptic sages.[5] The sultan was there, too, interested as he was in the outcome of this dialogue between East and West. Two opposing armies were arrayed outside in the summer sun, preparing themselves for battle while these men continued to talk, day after day. I like to think that they spoke of more profound issues than that of religious superiority. Surely Francis spoke to them of the beauty of poverty, and of the green land of Umbria that had nurtured his vision. Surely he alerted them to the value of a life lived outside the narrow confines of ownership and possession. His hosts, in turn, would have introduced him to a new level of understanding about the nature of remembrance (*dhikr*), and how important it is to invoke a divine Name until the endless repetition seals up the soul's energies to produce a state of ecstatic intoxication, similar to the repetition of the Jesus Prayer among Greek Orthodox *hesychasts*.

---

5. Sultan al-Kamil counted a number of Copts among his advisors. One assumes, therefore, that he was familiar with the tenets of Christianity from discussions with them.

I'm beginning to think that some of these ideas are part of the "treasure" that Francis returned to Umbria with under the cloak of his visionary imagination. He didn't speak of his meeting with the sages at the sultan's court precisely because what they had imparted to him was not communicable in the ordinary sense. They spoke of issues to do with breaking down the representational faculties in order to realize an entirely different level of sensory perception. Until this point, Francis had dealt with the symbols of his vocation, not least being the passion of Jesus Christ, its mysticism, and its regionalism in Palestine. He had come to the Holy Land in order to affirm his belief in the Crucifixion as a life-determining event in the history of humanity, and in the life of the individual. Among the Sufis of Egypt, however, he had discovered a more subtle symbolism at work: that of "oriental knowledge" (*ilim ishraqi*), a non-representative knowledge whose Latin equivalent is the expression *cogitio matutina*, meaning "morning knowledge." It is the knowledge that Saint Augustine intimated as an immediate presence of the Known, in a way that he who knows himself is present to himself. *Cogitio matutina* is to enter into the heaven of the soul, a condition that Francis was to finally experience at La Verna when he received the Stigmata five years later.

All this was imbedded in the Illuminist philosophy current in his time. It's no accident that almost immediately after his return to Italy in 1220 Francis abdicated his position as head of the brotherhood. Sick, tired, and tormented by a desire to devote the rest of his life to contemplation, Francis chose his own "path of the rose" in his bid to put into practice what he had learned in Egypt. He retired to Fonte Colombo and entered into a long period of meditation. Although, at this time, he was asked to write down the final Rule of the order, his heart wasn't in it. It took him many days to dictate even a few sentences. Reform was in the air, and his position as founder was little more than symbolic.

But Francis no longer cared. As Thomas of Celano relates, he wanted to "pass his time with God, and to shake off from himself any dust that might be clinging to him from his association with mankind." Francis had finally made his choice: to enter into that morning knowledge whose object was bliss.

Far from being an unsuccessful trip to the Holy Land as some chroniclers insist, I believe that Francis encountered something priceless there. Until this point his Christianity had been essentially Western in tenor, the result of centuries of careful determination of how and what a person should believe. To travel to the East is always going to be a life-changing event for any Christian, since Christianity is an "oriental" religion that draws its power from the morning sun, not the warm glow of sunset. The clarity and abstraction of morning gives to it a dimension that prefigures an affinity with the universality of spiritual experience. In a non-canonical gospel found in Nag Hammadi known as the Gospel of Philip, a gospel purporting to give additional information about the life of the Savior, Christ is called in Syriac *Pharisatha*, meaning "the one who is spread out." This, too, implies his universality in that it's said that he came to "crucify the world."

The idea of crucifying the world may well be what Francis had in mind as he prepared himself in the next few years for his encounter with the seraph at La Verna. It's no accident that the Stigmata is a form of world-crucifixion, a reiteration of a cosmic event and its subsequent powers of renewal. All his life Francis was aware of the burden that he carried on his shoulders. He knew that more was expected of him than simply to be a holy man. In a sense he had prepared himself to receive the wounds of a world already in conflict with itself. The old certainties were being undermined; the Church was in moral decline; the rise of medieval capitalism was drawing people away from simple acts of piety. They were beginning to take control of their lives in a way that had never happened before. Spiritual life was under threat to the point where men and women were in danger of losing their ability to discern the difference been *cogitio matutina* and *cogitio vespertina,* the knowledge of evening and of purely outward considerations. The Stigmata, for all its historical and mystical connotations, was still an act of receptivity, of bridging the gap between the world and its mystical origins.

I now see the importance of the Holy Land as the country of the imagination for Francis. One must visit it not only once but often if one is to understand how affected he may have been by the Orient's conception of spiritual knowledge. Until he had gone there he had relied on his three practical tenets of poverty, chastity, and obedience to help him live out the full spiritual life. But once he had returned from Egypt it seems that a new level of consciousness entered his thinking. Man must learn to withdraw from the super-substance of being in order to realize his essential nature. He must learn how to grapple with his love and longing for the perfect and complete discovery of the Father. Though the Father reveals Himself eternally, He has no wish to be known other than in His unsearchable, primordial being. It is only through His spirit that He provides people with the ability to conceive of Him, and to speak about Him.

Hence Francis's silence on the matter of his Holy Land visit. There was nothing much he could say. He had met with Muslims, Orthodox, Copts, heretics, and infidels, and many other sects and cults. He had spoken with theologians and Sufis. He may well have met hermits in the hills around Jerusalem. Everywhere he went he would have encountered men with a deep interest in the subtleties of mystical thinking, for this is a natural pastime in the East. People there, even today, are always interested in discussing the permutations of spiritual existence. And Francis, with his gift for attracting people of like mind, would have had no trouble seeking them out (or vice versa). Perhaps this is what becoming a crusader really meant to him. Although in his youth he may have wanted to fight the good fight, in maturity surely he must have discovered that the battle could not be won with either sword or shield.

When I observed in the museum in Assisi the gift that Sultan Malik gave to Francis as they parted, I know that it embodied much more than a passing fancy. The instrument after all was a scourging device, not exactly a normal kind of gift. Clearly, these men had more in common than is given credit. The divine nostalgia of God to be known in his solitude, an important Sufi concept, Francis would have likely understood and felt some sympathy with. All his life he had struggled with the emancipation of his being through the acquiescence of his will. The one thing he would learn, however, which would transform his life in five years time, was that it is not possible to see or speak to God except through inspiration, or from behind a veil, or through an angel (seraph) sent and authorized by Him. Though he would never have met the prominent Persian poet and contemporary, Jalalludin Rumi, one of his remarks would have struck a chord if he had heard it: "The physical form is of great importance; nothing can be done without the consociation of the form and the essence. However often you might sow a seed stripped of its pod, it will not grow; sow it with the pod, it will become a great tree. From this point of view the body [Brother Donkey] is fundamental and necessary for the realization of the divine intention....It is suffering that leads to success in every instance."[6] If these two poets should have ever met in their wanderings through the Holy Land, then surely they would have found much in common. Moreover, I'm certain that Francis would have

---

6. Mevlana Jalalludin Rumi, the greatest of Persian poets, was born in Balkh, Khorasan, in 1207 A.D. He lived much of his life in Konya, central Turkey. There, he wrote his most famous work, the *Mathnawi*. Among his many precepts was a desire to see all religions as one. He founded the Mevlana order of dervishes, known today as the "whirling dervishes."

delighted in one of Rumi's couplets celebrating his beloved Lady Poverty:

Everyone who desires nothing is your disciple:
He gains that which resembles no object.

Egypt, then, was less a place than an imaginative kingdom ruled by the hidden message of God. Francis had journeyed there to hear this message, and to deepen his understanding of *cogitio matutina,* of morning knowledge.

CHAPTER NINE

Eyeless in Gaza

✳

I n the Rieti Valley, on a hill overlooking the city of Rieti itself,
lies the monastery of Fonte Colombo. It is a small monastery surrounded by deep shade and a sense of peace. To walk
its cobbled pathways is to enter into the spirit of Francis himself,
for Fonte Colombo was one of his favorite retreats. He came here
in order to meditate and to pray whenever issues affecting his
brotherhood troubled him. Overlooking the expanse of this
glacierlike valley, he was able to ponder those moments of infini-
tude that he had been so privileged to experience. La Verna may
lie behind him, but the winged seraph was always on his mind.

I had gone there knowing that this was the place where Francis
had entered his final period of suffering. At every stage of his life
it seems that pain and enlightenment accompanied him. In those
last years before his death his body had succumbed to a number
of ailments, including dropsy, liver and stomach problems, cata-
racts, tuberculosis, and not least the continuing presence of the
wounds of the Stigmata itself. These needed to be washed and
bandaged almost daily. He was, in a way, a walking hospital case.
Still, he refused to give in to Brother Donkey's demands, not even
when a young monk suggested that his body should be rewarded
for the work it had done on Francis's behalf. "Rejoice, brother

body," he said, "and forgive me for, behold, I now gladly fulfill your desires. I hasten to give heed to your complaints." But it was all too late. As Thomas of Celano relates, Francis was "dead to the world," and its pleasures were no more than a "cross to him." In its place, the Stigmata shone forth from his flesh, reflecting what Thomas calls a "deeply set root sprouting forth from his mind."

This was the man who had founded an army of *poverelli* reaching across much of Europe. He had charmed kings, sultans, cardinals, and popes. Nobles and peasants had embraced his philosophy of absolute poverty in pursuit of that "deeply set root." He had unleashed a vital new perception of how a person might conduct his or her inner life in the face of growing material wealth. By his example, people could now find the courage to say "no" to the obvious temptations of a life lived in the shade of a temporality that had begun to question the value of eternity as an eschatological event. Francis, for all his commitment to the acquisition of nothingness, was a man who, through his own actions, embodied what lay buried in the word itself. The act of thinking oneself into a state where death was clearly on his mind as he lay on his bed of straw dealing with his various ailments and his approaching blindness.

Fonte Colombo is where he came to be cured at the insistence of others. That he could barely see, that his order had been overrun by reformists eager to soften some of his injunctions, that he lay there with the five wounds of Christ suppurating under their bandages—none of these issues were important to him. Ever since his return from Egypt he had abandoned any possibility of successfully dealing with the world. His brotherhood, for all its ideals and unlikely success, was no more than another fragile edifice built by men. All he had ever really done was to alert people to the possibility of attaining to spiritual enlightenment. The rocky road of abstinence and pain, hunger and extreme poverty, solitude and prayer, these were the true artifacts effecting the realization of the dying God within. Francis had chosen this path above all others. He had tried to share it. In the end he couldn't force others to travel with him beyond the emptiness of the world simply because he chose to do so himself.

Less than two years before his death he finally submitted to the pope's doctors, who happened to be in Rieti where Honorius III was briefly living in exile from Rome after riots supporting the faction headed by his own brother had forced him to leave. Francis probably didn't feel the need for an operation on his eyes, but others did so on his behalf. In those days it was believed that cauterizing his head "in several places" would release the poison behind his eyes. The operation was simple but painful: hot irons were placed about the temple to sear away the illness. Francis was subjected to bleeding and the application of ointments to his eyes. None of these ministrations worked. He lay on his rough bed, in a room overlooking the valley, dealing with a head that was on fire from his wounds. No only did he have those of the Stigmata to contend with, but now those inflicted by well-meaning court physicians. The irony of his situation couldn't have escaped him, I feel sure: the wounds of Christ must have been far easier to deal with than the ones inflicted by his friends.

For my own part, I wanted to spend time in that room where the operation had occurred. It is bare now save for a chair beside a small fireplace. One door leads off into a bedroom. Yet time has not erased Francis's presence. He lies there, barely able to make out the roof beams above his head, while four loyal brothers administer to his needs.[1] Does he recall the moment a few years before when he was inspired by a dream to write down his precious Rule? He who understood the power of images certainly

---

1. These brothers, though not named by Thomas of Celano in order "to spare their modesty," were later discovered to be Angelo Tancredi, Brother Rufino, Brother Leo, and Brother John of Lodi.

must have realized the importance of his dream when he awoke. As Thomas of Celano later relates:

> IT SEEMED TO HIM *that he had to gather the finest crumbs of bread from the ground, and to distribute them to the many hundreds of hungry brothers who were standing around him. But while he was afraid to distribute such small crumbs lest such minute particles of dust should fall from his hands, a voice spoke to him from above: "Francis, make one host out of all the crumbs and give it to those who want to eat it." When he did this, those who did not receive devoutly, or who despised the gift they had received, were soon seen to be greatly infected with leprosy. The saint told all these things to his companions in the morning, regretting that he did not understand the mystery of the vision. But after a little while, while he continued to keep watch in prayers, a voice came down to him from Heaven: "Francis," it said, "the crumbs of last night are the words of the gospel, the host is the rule, the leprosy is wickedness."*

✳

Thus was his final testament to his brethren pronounced in a dream. The crumbs of his thought must be kneaded into a cogent rule for all men to live by. With great difficulty, and aided by a scribe, he managed to record his thoughts in a document of nearly two thousand words. It is no mystical tract, but a careful articulation of how to live a devout life. "Let all brothers be clothed in mean garments....Friars are to fast from the feast of All Saints to the Nativity [Christmas]....No brother is to do evil or speak evil to another....Be always busy in some good work....Beware of traipsing through the world for any filthy lucre....Let them remain silent whenever God gives them the grace....It is not lawful to ride horseback unless constrained by infirmity...." On and on it goes, laying down the law of a narrow but complete life. To enter into such a life is to make a compact with denial. Its outcome? I had to go back to Francis's remarks about joy in order to understand. As Thomas of Celano writes:

AND IF LATER, suffering intensely from hunger and the painful cold, with night falling, we still knock [on the door of a monastery], and crying loudly beg them to open for us and let us come in for the love of God, and he [a monk] grows still more angry and says: "Those fellows are bold and shameless ruffians. I'll give them what they deserve!" And he comes out with a knotty club, and grasping us by the cowl, throws us onto the ground, rolling us in the mud and snow, and beats us with the club so much that he covers our bodies with wounds—if we endure all these evils and insults and blows with joy and patience, that is perfect joy.

※

Once again I am confronted with Francis's love of inversion. Here joy is associated with abnegation, with abuse, with exclusion. The man is not satisfied with good works as a measure of what a man is or might be; he wants to see him humiliated for the sake of joy. It sounds like an extreme masochism is at work: Francis wants to invoke happiness out of the reduction of a man to his most basic attributes. Man must become the butt of ridicule, despised for his inadequacies, spurned for his allegiance to poverty. True joy, it seems, can only be achieved by existing outside the norms of human conduct. His idea of joy is so complete that it aspires to a wretchedness without recourse, and the realization of a magisterial failure. What he wants to do is continually reopen old wounds, those wounds of the Stigmata. He wants to be dazzled and crushed at the same time by the brilliance and the ungraspable nature of that ineffable light of the seraph.

How could a man do this to himself, I asked? It was a question, I suppose, forever on my mind as I wandered about Umbria in search of Francis. It was hard to imagine a man being so ruthless with himself. Christ had never asked this of his disciples, nor had he practiced such extreme acts of self-mortification. The most he ever did was fast forty days in the wilderness. Except for his crucifixion, at no time did he incur the violence of others or of himself. In comparison Christ was a benign figure whose only act of violence was to throw the moneychangers out of the temple. So why did Francis think that his own example mirrored that of the Savior?

I have no clear answer. I only know that his asceticism holds a fascination for us even today. In order to understand its origins, one has to go back to at least to the fourth century and explore the numerous Gnostic sects that had sprung up throughout the Middle East, Greece, Bulgaria, and later Bosnia. Known as Messalians or Euchites (the "Praying Men"), they believed in a lower world of darkness and a higher world of light. For these people, the world was the devil's handiwork, and everything—matter, flesh, and the human soul—was impregnated with diabolical substance. The devil was physically and psychically present in each person. The task of every human being was to eradicate the demon living parasitically within by using particular ascetical techniques.

For the Euchites, perpetual prayer enabled them to generate an outpouring of spirit at every moment of the day, which in turn plunged them into a second state that opened their souls to an influx of the Holy Spirit, and so liberated them from the devil forever. Through incantatory prayer a spiritual battle was waged. For this purpose, the Euchites chose the Lord's Prayer, which they recited endlessly to the point of vertigo, stimulating themselves by dancing and imbibing concoctions. In this way they attained to a state of ecstasy, during the course of which the destruction of the devil took place. Known as the "Lazy Men" because of their avoidance of all manual work, they slept in the open air and begged for food. They were always on the move, and never resisted those who challenged their beliefs. Of necessity, they would submit to baptism, take communion, and make confession if they thought these acts might be seen as a sufficient demonstration of their contrition. Like Francis, they had no problem in inverting every argument if they felt it might conceal their real motives.

In some ways Francis's behavior mirrored the practices of these Euchites. Of course, it is unlikely that he had ever met such people, but he may well have been influenced by their doctrine, then very much "in the air" during his lifetime. It seems to me, too, that his peripatetic behavior he may have inadvertently copied from the Euchites and the Bogamils of Serbia and Bosnia. Wandering, by its very nature, is a denial of cultural norms and the sedentary activity that defines social boundaries. Even today we look upon gypsies with suspicion simply because they show no respect for the value of place. They, like the Euchites, like Francis, draw their inspiration from the continuity of stories, the history of families, the rich tapestry of memory. The primary value of experience takes precedence over that of property, the conglomeration of estates, or the amassing of capital. It is no wonder that men like Francis, and like his counterparts among the Euchites, threaten the stability of a region. They carry their culture with them rather than implant it in the earth in the form of buildings, town squares, or the age-old repository of lore that lies under the roof of any cathedral or village church. Blindness to a wanderer, therefore, is the hardest scourge to bear.

In a tiny chapel that I discovered below the monastery at Fonte Colombo I found a fresco depicting Francis receiving the Rule of 1221. It is a scene that echoes a woodcut in the main chapel above, where Francis is on his knees in the presence of God on high. A scribe sits to his left, taking down the precious words of this revolutionary mode of conduct. The chapel is filled with the agony of creation, and of a man's desperation to get it down right. If nothing else, Francis wanted to make sure that those who succeeded him would not subvert his allegiance to absolute poverty. "I, Brother Francis," he dictated, "firmly command and enjoin that of the things that are written in this Life no one shall subtract or add. Nor shall the brothers have any other Rule." It is the cry of one who know the tide of events has already turned against him.

I felt deeply for Francis. He knew that he stood for the highest ideal known to humankind—that of pursuit of perfection, the realization of the Perfect Man. This was a truly Christian ideal. No one in the West had promulgated the idea with such acuity and depth, not even Plato or the pre-Socratic philosophers. It may be argued that the Buddhist vision intimated such a possibility in the attainment of Nirvana. But such a concept had never been fully articulated in the various religions throughout the Middle East prior to Christianity. The Zoroastrians had avoided the concept altogether, except as an appendage to their dualist beliefs pertaining to a battle between light and darkness. Francis, on the other hand, had made the idea central to his beliefs.

The Perfect Man could only be realized by an active pursuit of will-lessness, of what Heidegger called "releasement." Such a condition goes beyond the distinction between activity and passivity, because releasement doesn't belong to the domain of the will at all. It lies in the region of the *poverty* of will. One has to go back to Meister Eckhart to find an explanation of this rather difficult concept, a concept that asks God to negate "Himself" in our lives: "If we are to be poor in will, then we must will and desire as little as we willed and desired before we came into being. It is in this way that someone is poor who wills nothing….Therefore we should be utterly free of self-knowledge as we were before we were created, that we should allow God to do what he will and that we should be entirely free of all things." In other words, the

Perfect Man harks back to a time before self-consciousness and willfulness motivated his actions.

I suspect it was this idea that embodied Francis's insistence on the absolute value of poverty. He clung to it more than he did any other. He pleaded its cause against the reformists in his own order, against the papacy, against every institution that wanted to soften its impact in his Rule.[2] He knew that poverty implied will-lessness, releasement, and a condition that was so solitary and unencumbered that a man would not necessarily know whether it was God who acted through him. Poverty was not simply a state of physical want, but rather one of a lack in spirit and a lack in knowing. A true *poverello* has no knowledge of anything, neither of God nor creatures nor himself. He is one who desires not to know or perceive anything of God's works. As a *poverello*, he is one who longs to be poor in knowing.

We must return to Meister Eckhart for a clearer explanation. According to him, a poor man is someone who possesses nothing, even the idea of not possessing anything. Further, he is not a person who wishes to perform God's will. He lives in such a way as to be free of both his own will and of God's will, and so be as he was when he was first created. According to Eckhart, this is the highest poverty. A poor person is also someone who knows nothing of the action of God within him. Purest poverty is attained when someone is free of all knowledge and perception.

Eckhart goes further and describes what he calls the "ultimate poverty." Let him tell us in his own words:

---

2. The actions of the reformers needs to be clarified. One of them, Brother Pietro Staccia, set up a house of studies at the University of Bologna, which was famous for its commentaries on Roman civil law. When Francis arrived there one day, he repudiated Staccia, cursed him, and drove out the brothers resident in it. Staccia begged Francis to lift his curse but he refused, maintaining that Christ himself had confirmed its justice. It is said that shortly afterwards, Pietro Staccia "gave up his life to the devil, surrounded by a horrible stench."

I HAVE OFTEN SAID, as great masters have said, that we should be so free of all things and of all works, both inner and outer, that we become the place where God can act. But now we put it differently. If it is the case when someone is free of all creatures, of God and of themselves, if God finds a place to act in them, then we say: as long as this exists in someone, they have not reached the ultimate poverty. For God does not intend that there be a place in someone where he can act, but if there is to be true poverty of spirit, someone must be so free of God and all his works that if God wishes to act in the soul, he must himself be the place in which he can act, and this he is certainly willing to be free. For if God finds us this poor, then God performs his own active work, and we receive God in ourselves, and God becomes the place of his work since God works within himself. In this poverty, we attain again the eternal being which we once enjoyed....[3]

✳

I can't help feeling that this is what Francis was driving at in his concept of poverty. He wanted to be so free of God, so spiritually poverty-stricken, that he might become the passive receptacle for God's work. His severe asceticism was a way of making his body into that receptacle. He identified physical abnegation with *apathea*, with will-lessness. It may be argued that he devoted too much of his energy to breaking the body when his real task was to pacify the willfulness of the mind. But I suspect in the end he regarded willfulness as belonging to both the body and the mind. More importantly, the poverty that he spoke of as being so important to the conduct of a life possessed a significance that for the most part has escaped the notice of commentators. For him,

✳ ───────

3. This remarkable excerpt can be found in Sermon 22 of Meister Eckhart's *Se-* *lected German Sermons.* Penguin Classics.

poverty was a manifestation of God's Nothingness, his deep Unknowableness.

No wonder the Rule became such a difficult document to realize. It is said that Francis spent many days working on the project, sometimes gleaning only one or two sentences from his thoughts each session. Fonte Colombo became the husk in which the seed was brought to fruition. Each sentence was wrung out of his conviction that no compromise should be made with the basic tenets that he had devised back in 1210, when he had written a draft of the first Rule. The document itself is fraught with tension. On the one hand, he is at pains to recommend a way of life right down to the minutest detail; on the other, he wants nothing more than to break into a paean of joy celebrating the presence of God in his life. I detect beneath the cover of words a desire to articulate the "ultimate poverty" that Eckhart spoke of. In the end, unable to contain himself, he broke out of the prison of legalism that he had been forced to confine himself in for some thousands of words, and made his final plea for the divine sanctity of will-lessness. Only this, he believed, would stem the tide of the reformers and justify the continued existence of the brotherhood as he had conceived it originally.

Surely Eckhart would have approved of the power and lyricism of Francis's attempt to convey what was his destiny to experience a few years later at La Verna. One can almost hear the seraph's voice at work as he relates the final aspiration of a man dedicated to understanding the deeper workings of God.

LET ALL OF US EVERYWHERE, in every place, at every hour, and every season, daily and constantly, truly and humbly believe and hold in our hearts, and love, honor, adore, serve, praise and bless, glorify and exalt, magnify and render thanks to the most High and Supreme Eternal God, Trinity and Unity, the Creator of all and the Savior of all who be-

lieve and hope in Him and love Him who, without begin-
ning and without end, is unchangeable, unseen, indescrib-
able, ineffable, incomprehensible, unfathomable, blessed,
praiseworthy, glorious, exalted above all, sublime, most high,
gentle, lovable, delightful, and wholly desirable above all
else, forever.

✳

Surely these remarks confirm Francis's desire to pour out his heart in one prolonged act of superlatives. The poet in him was being undermined by the glorious negativity of Deity itself. At the same time, one feels that Francis was always in control of what he wanted to say. His life of asceticism and total commitment to trying to understand the simplicity and nakedness of being had opened up for him his own inner ground. Now he was able to stand in it, in the abysm of his aloneness, and utter to himself what Saint Augustine so ably expressed when explaining the necessity for the soul to transcend itself: "I have poured my soul *over* myself." Francis, I suspect, saw in these words of his Rule the final act of immersion in his own soul. It was a view echoed a few years later by the Franciscan poet, Jacopone da Todi, in one of his poems:

No man can taste the fruit of this glorious nihil.
If not led by the hand of God; of himself he can do nothing

O Glorious state, in the quiet center of the void
The intellect and the emotions at rest!

So that when he lay in the room in agony after his cauterization, all his real suffering was behind him. The eyes of his mind had not yet been blinded. He could still see with the piercing glance of one who understood God *as* his suffering. He could see, too, as a man who had finally learned how to transcend his humanity. For this was his great achievement: by a monumental act of self-negation he had managed to dismantle the meaning of being human in order to realize its innermost kernel. Yes, even his humanity had to be abandoned if he were to achieve complete annihilation of self. As Eckhart said, "Whoever desires to be given everything, must first give everything away." His body, his mind, and his sight were but offerings on his part. We must go to a Moorish philosopher, Ibn Tufail, who died a few years after Francis's birth, and who wrote extensively on the idea of the Perfect Man in his parable *The Story of Hay ibn Yaqzan,* to understand the spiritual transformation that he underwent: "The heaven and the earth and all that lies between them vanished from his thoughts and his memory. So also did spiritual visions, bodily forces, and all the non-material forces that are the essences conscious of that Being which is Truth; and his own essence vanished with them. All became scattered as dust, shrunk, vanished. Only the Truth, the One, the Being whose existence is permanent, remained." I am sure this is how Francis must have felt as he lay on his bed of straw, contemplating what was left of his life in this world.

On the path outside the main chapel I happened to pass by the ossuary lying among its foundations. A window opened into a shadowy cavern. Peering inside, I noticed a pile of bones, skulls, and partly clad tibia and fibula in contorted arrangements. I felt a strange sensation: to witness literally layers of monks' bones, all of them formed and fashioned by a lifetime of prayer and asceticism, was to begin to understand the nature of Francis's legacy. He had given to these men, generations of them, a rule to live by. He had given them a reason for submitting their bodies and minds to the tortuous business of physical suffering. Most of all, he had made it possible for Western spirituality to reinvent itself as a viable force in the battle against materialism. Let there be no mistake: this battle had to be fought and won if European sensibility was not to fall back upon the illusory assumption that belief-in-itself was all it required to maintain its existence.

I came away from Fonte Colombo that day knowing I had finally begun to understand Francis. The light of his personality was beginning to shine in me at last. He was a spiritual genius, yes; but he was also a man deeply afflicted by self-doubt. The difference between his self-doubt and my own, however, could not be bridged, so great was the gap that he had opened up by way of his example. Alone among medieval ascetics he had discovered a way of approaching Deity that overcame the objectivity of God which had served Christians so well until this point. He had managed to implant God in himself.

CHAPTER TEN

Brother Sun
Sings

✳

Thomas of Celano relates how Francis was deeply entranced by the written language. He was often so overcome by joy when he heard the holy Name pronounced that he found it hard to contain himself. Thomas said that Francis felt like a "new man," one who had come "from another world" whenever he encountered the beauty of language. If he found anything written on a piece of paper lying on the ground or abandoned in a house, whether it was about God or any other subject, he would pick it up with the greatest reverence and put it in a safe place. When asked one day why he so diligently collected these scraps of paper, often containing the writings of pagans with no mention of the name of the Lord on them, he replied: "Brother, each of these letters may one day be used to make up the glorious name of Jesus Christ. Whatever is good in these words doesn't pertain to pagans alone but to God, to whom belongs everything good." He even refused to delete letters if his scribe had wrongly placed them in a word. It seems the alphabet was his bulwark.

There is a long tradition of the mystical properties of letters. It is said that among the Jews of Provence and Spain there flowered a current of Hebrew mysticism destined to have a profound influence on Europe's search for a perfect language. This was known as the kabbala, an esoteric tradition originally transmitted orally by adepts that regarded creation itself as a linguistic phenomenon. It was preeminently a technique of reading and interpreting sacred text. A kabbalist scholar sought to discover an eternal text underneath that of the written Torah. This he believed to be created by God before all the worlds, and consigned to his angels. The primordial Torah was often described as being inscribed in black flames upon white fire.

Such a tradition inevitably leads to language being considered as a symbolic instrument. It no longer stood for a relationship between an object and its expression, or that of a world represented merely by referring to it, as it had been in the philosophical tradition of Europe since Aristotle. Rather, the kabbalists believed that if God created the world by uttering sounds, or by combining written letters, it must follow that these elements were not representations of preexisting things, but were the very forms by which the elements of the universe were molded. The language of creation is perfect not because it happened to reflect the structure of the universe in some exemplary fashion, but because it actually created the universe.

I suspect this was how Francis must have felt about his own language, none other than his Italo-Umbrian dialect in which he normally conversed. Some years later, Dante was to describe it as *volgare,* and to dream of making it more *illustre*—that is, more illustrious, in the sense of "shining with light." He longed to transform *volgare* into a language capable of dealing with government, law, and philosophy. He even envisaged it one day being spoken by kings in the royal courts of Italy. But until then—until he had written his *Divine Comedy,* at least—the language of curial activity would remain that of Latin. This is how it was in Francis's day, too.

Curiously, Dante also believed that language, or a woman anyway, first uttered words, in this case Eve when she spoke to the serpent. As good a chauvinist as he was, Dante found himself troubled that "an act so noble for the human race did not come from the lips of a man, but rather from those of a woman." Adam went on to name the animals, but the vital act of linguistic behavior had been performed nonetheless. It was woman who uttered the first word, and man only later who laid down the rules of language. Such an act made it imperative that language becomes a male preserve in the interest of sexual dominance. The fire of expression must remain in the hands of men, it seems.

It is understandable, therefore, why Francis treated the written word with such reverence. His knowledge of troubadour poetry meant that he was heir to a long tradition derived from Spain and Provence, which may have reinforced his belief in the mystical properties of language. God could be "constructed" by way of letters. His ineffability could be re-sounded, even if it couldn't be understood. Further, God could be celebrated in poetry and the various tracts that he so carefully composed during his ministry. Indeed, it is not so surprising to find that Francis resorted to writing his final testament on his deathbed in which he continued to reiterate his central themes on the holy life. He is believed to have begun it in the bishop's palace in Assisi, before being brought back to Santa Maria degli Angeli at Portiuncula to die. Visited by a physician from Arezzo, he was told that his death would come towards the end of September or the fourth of October. So this document was his way of welcoming the arrival of Sister Death.

In the testament, he begins to reveal personal aspects of his life for the first time. We discover, for example, that his early dislike of lepers ultimately led him to attach himself to Christ. We hear from his own lips of his loyalty to priests and clerics, whether or not they might be more influenced by worldly concerns than those of the spirit. "I see nothing with my bodily eyes of Him who is the most high Son of God except his most holy Body and most holy Blood, which I receive when they alone administer to others," he said, defending their role of offering the Host during Mass even if they were in a state of sin. Most of all, his testament represents one last attempt by him to set in stone his vision of a life lived in poverty. One could say that he had become obsessional about the issue.

So it is not surprising to find him writing poetry whenever he felt a strong desire to express his personal sense of joy. The troubadour in him was never far away from the austere ascetic, it seems. I always have the feeling that Francis was torn between being a pedant, a guru, or holy man, and that of a man addicted to verbal expression for its own sake. For the most part, language became a vehicle of exhortation, an ideogram to invoke lost innocence. He used it with one purpose in mind: to draw people back into a loving relationship with their Maker. But in the end, even he found this too limiting. He wanted to break out of the carapace that he had allowed himself to be surrounded by so as to celebrate the wonder of the world in his own unique fashion.

We do not know how many poems he wrote during his lifetime. He may have merely memorized them rather than put them to paper. But we do know that in his last days he composed one of the most poignant and beautiful poems to appear in the Italian language—and one of the first. *The Canticle of Brother Sun* is a paean to the wonder of existence, to the immeasurability of God's presence in the world. It was the final statement of a man who had tasted every joy, experienced every form of agony, and known every depth to which a man might descend in order to arrive at his own inner ground. The Canticle is less a poem than it is a confession of inadequacy on the part of Francis. He probably felt that in writing it he might have even cheated Sister Death.[1]

✳ ————————

1. The poem was written in the garden attached to the monastery of San Damiano, when he was in the care of Clare and her nuns.

Most high, omnipotent, good Lord
To you alone belongs praise and glory
Honor, and blessing. No man
Is worthy to breathe your name.

My Lord, be praised for all your creatures
Especially Brother Sun, who gives us
The day that through you illuminates us.
Beautiful is he, and radiant with splendor
Your gravest witness, O Omnipotent One.

My Lord, be praised for Sister Moon
And every star made so brightly, precious
Beautiful in this your heaven.

My Lord, be praised for Brother Wind
Clear skies and cloudy in all weather
So life-giving, be praised.

My Lord, be praised for Sister Water
So necessary, so humble, precious, and chaste.

My Lord, be praised for Brother Fire
He who lights up the night
So carefree, robust, and fierce.

My Lord, be praised for our sister, Mother Earth
Who nourishes and watches over us
With fruits abundant as her variety of flowers.

As far as we know the poem's first public performance was at the
bishop's palace in the presence of both the bishop and the excom-
municated mayor. The latter had earned Bishop Guido's ire after
a quarrel between the two. Francis asked the brothers to sing the
poem in front of these men in the hope of reconciling them. For
good measure, he added a couple more verses to touch their hearts:

My Lord, be praised by those whose
Forgiveness is inspired by your love
Praise and bless the Lord
Give him thanks, with all humility
For those who suffer so.

It is said that both men forgave one another immediately, setting an example for other bitterly fought disputes between Church and commune, between the partisans of pope and emperor, between one town and the next. The Canticle had achieved its first victory: the reconciliation of men who had all but forgotten their inheritance. The earth was there to laud, not to argue over.

Francis added three more verses after his doctors had told him that there was nothing more they could do for him. It was almost as if, by inserting a paean to Sister Bodily Death, he had made his peace with cessation. Far from cheating her, he now welcomed her as his savior. She alone had the power to take him up into that cloud of unknowing he had sought all his life.

My Lord, be praised through our Sister Bodily Death
From whom no living man escapes.

Woe to those who die in mortal sin!
Bless those she finds doing your holy will
For the second death will not harm them.

My Lord, be praised and blessed
We give thanks, and with humility serve you.

In this poem alone Francis had answered his critics. It represents the distillation of a life. He had become nothing more than a living act of praise, a laud at one with the world that made him. Few poets ever scale these heights. Few poets can match his loftiness. He had transformed all of nature into a cosmic prayer. We must go as far back as the Greek tragedians or forward to Shakespeare to hear its like. *The Canticle of Brother Sun* is an attempt to anthropomorphize Deity by attributing to it natural characteristics that become values. The earth becomes a retort in which all of nature is reduced to its essence: nothing less than an attempt to magnify, and so make visible, the imperceptible structure of Deity itself. In his Canticle, Francis wanted to go beyond language and so negate what Adam had codified.

One must be clear about this. Francis was uniquely conscious of the unity of the universe. In so doing, he was able to retrace Deity's mysterious whorl of existence back to a center that he believed it had invented to occupy the void. He had reached a point, too, when he realized that he was little more than a creature of severance who could no longer resist, even at the end, a desire to cut off the limbs of all those false words, which had shaped and intoxicated him throughout his life.

Any place that a man chooses to die becomes a source of anguish. Perhaps Francis thought that by writing down his poem he might be saved by words from experiencing the full horror of this "non-place." Life for him had become porous, and suggested death without the comfort of composition. He had no choice but to accept that each page of his poem was coated with undeniable night. By articulating his wonder, and rendering his thanks, he made it possible for human beings no longer to be responsible for the death of God, nor for God to be responsible for the death of human beings. A dangerous game, indeed; but one that Francis had played for much of his life. Was it any wonder that he never tested the authority of the Church by public accusation, when in reality he was doing so by his every action and in his private utterances? For those who condemn him for not taking on the corruption of the Church at that time, let them remember the nature, and the risk, of the path he had chosen for himself.

The path of the rose is as it suggests: the beauty of unparalleled blooms protected by the thorns of circumstance. Francis had tried to forge a spirituality from an extreme asceticism matched by a reverence for the beauty of ecstatic experience. Alone among men, he had bridged the gap between the asocial life of an anchorite in the desert and the more inward dispensation of the monastic orders of his time. As far as he was concerned it was not good for a monk to quit the world altogether, nor was it of any value to society for men to gather in monasteries without sharing their spiritual largesse. He had founded his brotherhood as a lay brotherhood that lived in the community. In fact, it relied directly on the community to survive. Begging, as we know, was the only way for a brother to eat. Each friar depended on the good will and tacit support of everyone in the community. His spirituality was nourished directly by all those who revered his presence in their midst.

In this sense, the Franciscan brotherhood possessed far more popular appeal than the larger orders, which regarded themselves as bastions of spirituality rather than its nurturers. In his own lifetime Francis saw his order grow from the original twelve to numbers exceeding five thousand. Every member of his community was expected to interact with society in some way, yet at the same time maintain his distance. A fruitful tension emerged between a grass-roots spirituality that satisfied popular expectations, and the maintenance of the principle of strict ascetic practice and solitary retreat by the brothers themselves. They, in turn, became the conscience of society without incurring its disapprobation. The Franciscan emerged as a counterweight to the emerging materialism inspired by a new mercantile class.

Francis was one of the first to use the language of the people to spread his message. He more or less spurned Latin as his medium of communication. When one thinks that Latin was the universal language of the Church, and that all theology was written down in this ancient juridical language, it is easy to see why he felt that official learning might contaminate the minds of his followers. To resort to Latin was to go over to the enemy so far as he was concerned. Latin was the language of doctrine, dialectic, and hierarchy. The supreme pontiff, the pope himself, continued to promulgate all dogma in the ancient imperial language of Rome. I suspect it was a conscious decision on Francis's part to reject Latin precisely for this reason. He had no wish to align his brotherhood with a concept of hierarchy that reflected the anti-democratic tenor he had struggled so hard to resist all his life. Latin was the language of spiritual oppression; Italian was the language of freedom and ecstatic experience. In his letter to Anthony of Padua at the time when the younger man had been asked to teach theology to the brothers in Bologna a few years before his death, one can sense an ambivalence in Francis's remarks:

> To Brother Anthony, my "bishop" [his quotes], Brother Francis sends his greetings.
>
> It pleases me that you read sacred theology to the friars, provided that amid such study you do not extinguish the rule of prayer and devotion, as is contained in the Rule.

*

Clearly, Francis was not entirely happy with developments in Bologna. But he acquiesced, provided that the brothers might be brought back to the simplicity of the Rule, expressed as it was in Italian, not in Latin. It has been argued that parenthesizing Anthony's title as "bishop" was a manifestation of his esteem for the young theologian. But it may also have been a way of warning Anthony of the dangers of his intended occupation. Beware of the wiles of Latin, he seemed to be inferring. Stay close to the humble dialectic of the Rule.

It's no accident that Francis asked his brothers to sing his Canticle before the mayor and bishop. He actually believed in the power of language to change people's hearts. Though it doesn't bear comparison, one thinks of Pericles' speech before the Athenian assembly and his bid to defend the *demos*—that is, the ordinary people—at a time when the city was threatened by the Delian league. Both men in their own way felt that they could convert people through argument. The similarity ends in that Pericles did not use poetry as his vehicle. On the other hand, Francis really did think that the shape and beauty of a poem might achieve a positive outcome. One must scour history to find another example of a poem being used to settle a public dispute.

So the Canticle is more than just a poem. It is an attempt to subvert God's absence through the use of language. If we look back at all the poetry of history until this point, we are reminded of its importance as a powerful narrative tool, and to some extent an incantatory device. Men from Homer onwards used poetry to express their deepest emotions about the tribe. *Istoria* was embodied in the poem. Once framed by stanza and verse, the tribe's memories attained to mythic status. Poetry became in this instance the language of the gods.

What Francis did was to transform the poem's role. Instead of being tagged to a people's history, he saw another entirely new dimension for it to express. He realized that writing a poem was alien to the current ideals and ideas that his people might have about the world. He realized, too, that the infinite could never serve as a background for communication, nor eternity, while it remained congealed in myth. Somehow the poem must be used in a different way. It must effect the idea that life is a gift from beyond, a gift which death bestows upon the individual in order that he might match this image within himself. The poem became the nexus between person and Maker. It mirrored the sheer stubbornness that existed between these two, so long as each saw one another as an object outside him. Francis wanted the poem to overreach this age-old contumacy. Job's problematic relationship with Yahweh must be made a thing of the past. From now on, God and His people must stand on an equal footing.

In his Canticle we are confronted with the entire cosmos being compressed into a singular arrangement of words. They have been carefully crafted to reflect the idea that God inhabits all things, that he exists as an atomization in the physical world. Pantheism? Particularly theologians fearful of where his unabashed praise of nature might lead them have leveled it at Francis on more than one occasion. Could the Church, which was an institution founded upon doctrinal authority and the power of hierarchy, survive such statements? Could it allow itself to be undermined by such an unadorned celebration of physis? Would the idea of a metaphysical reality devolve into a recognition of its oppressive nature while it continued to remain in the Church's hands? These were questions that arose out of the Canticle. It was an incendiary poem. It threatened everything that the Church stood for. Indeed, it is notable that at no point in the poem did Francis refer to his beloved Church. The Canticle had erased institutional religious authority simply by ignoring it.

More than anything, I think that Francis wanted to give expression to the impossible dream of life. Something inside told him that the world of physis could not be denied. All his life he had attempted to do so, of course. His asceticism was a testimony to his fear of succumbing to what he believed was an agent of the devil. But at the last, when he lay ill and dying at San Damiano in the care of Clare and her sisters, he suddenly came to terms with his principle dilemma: that of denuding his body of its senses in a bid to *escape that body*. This is what he had practiced, and this is what led him to recognize the futility of trying to waste away for the sake of partaking in the pleasure of ecstatic experience. While he had clearly done so, it appears that it had been at some considerable cost. His order was already beginning to fragment because many refused to believe that the effort was worthwhile.

So the big question that the Canticle raises is this: should physis be demeaned for the sake of some hoped-for relationship with God? Do people need to have a one-on-one dialogue with their Maker? Is this, in fact, the result of the entire history of consciousness moving toward something intensely personal at the cost of the more open, free nature of the primordial that Meister Eckhart spoke of? Certainly some might think so. The argument Francis had with himself throughout his life centered on his disenchantment with material existence. For reasons best known to himself, he associated it with a falling away from being. From his viewpoint, man's destiny was to make more complex the nature of being, and so realize, once and for all, someone more perfectly endowed. Such a condition however was founded upon its antithesis: that man must return to a state of innocence. So now we know why Francis inverted every value; he wanted to unleash the innocent in himself, which had been chained for too long to his selfhood.

Each time I reread the *Canticle of Brother Sun*, I know that I am in the presence of a remarkable human being. The poem's breathless reach suggests a mind in league with its own contradiction. The world is out there, a wondrous encounter, a cherished orb of radiance and splendor. It is made up of wind, sky, flowers, the sun and moon, water, earth, night and day, everything that contributes to the secret murmurings of the cosmos. While lurking below the surface of this beauty and terror is Sister Bodily Death, preparing her magic potion. Cessation is her elixir, the sharp blade of her scythe. Francis knows this. He understands why she is doing what she does. He awaits the cup that she has prepared for him. He hangs on her every word, knowing that what she says holds no fear for him any more. The "second death" that she offers him is of no importance when compared to the one he has undergone at his own behest.

CHAPTER ELEVEN

Welcome, Sister Death

✳

I f it is true that God, death, and man attain eternity together, then Francis understood more than most his own march toward oblivion. Though he could not conceive of liberty without life, I think he knew that death was the only true act of liberation. His nature was always about invoking the paradox, the inversion. He liked to think that he put every moment of his life to good use celebrating it. At the same time he was the first to subject his body to a prolonged wound, which ultimately would turn out to be fatal. He knew that in death he would go back to the beginning of creation, and so resurrect the idea that although born in time he was nonetheless a creature of eternity.

At forty-four, he wasn't an old man. His ministry was barely eighteen years in the making. By any stretch of the imagination, he still had much to do. But I think that after the events of La Verna, he felt there was little left for him to achieve in this life. Bearing the wounds of the Stigmata must have been painful, even if they did render him in the image of Christ. Golgotha's legacy, as deeply transfiguring as it had been to him, could not remain in the sphere of the world for too long. It must be made to slip back into the preserve of history, an act of physical desecration that rendered sacrifice into one of the supreme gestures of forgiveness which man might bestow. For indeed, at this moment in time, Christ was manifestly a suffering man—and Francis knew it.

So his need to identify with Christ overruled all other considerations. We know, for example, that he asked his brothers to read from the Gospel of Saint John, detailing Christ's acceptance of his own death six days before the Passover.[1] The metaphor of a God-man preparing for his hour of death was attractive to Francis. The martyr in him had always wanted to die for the sins of others, however much he might have wished to deny it. Francis was like a man walking a tightrope. He enjoyed the idea of treading a line supported by two levels of reality. On the one hand there was the physical world that he had abandoned; on the other, the whitely lit expanse of the seraphim, and the satisfaction of knowing that at least once in his life he had managed to penetrate its mystery.

This is not to demean Francis—far from it. Rather, it raises him to the complexity of a man destined to be a saint. To presume that his innocence was a gift, when in fact he had created it for himself, says a great deal about his ability to refashion his identity and his conviction in the mold of the man he admired most. Or should I say "God"? Because either way he had proved that it was possible to live in the image of another. One is therefore in the presence of a living image of grace, a man who had sacrificed his self in the interest of that innocence he so yearned for.

After his sojourn at Fonte Colombo, his last year of life was characterized by his usual restlessness. Weighed down by his ail-

---

1. John 13:1: "It was before the feast of the Passover, and Jesus knew that the hour had come for him to pass from this world to the Father. He had always loved those who were his in the world, but now he showed how perfect his love was."

ments, he managed to reach La Foresta in the Rieti Valley where he retired into a cave to escape the light that so troubled his eyes. Like a mole he lived there, appearing only after sunset. When asked whether he didn't get bored with his present inactivity and his almost continuous suffering, he replied: "How can I be bored when I'm suffering all the time?" Pain had become his principal diversion. Any thought of experiencing another La Verna was now out of the question. Instead, he was buried in the bitterness of the garden of olives. Even his body was beginning to become public property: his nail clippings, hair, and the water in which he bathed were quickly taken away by his followers to be made into relics. It seemed that holy martyrdom was within his reach.

Sanctity is a heady concoction. Word soon spread that Francis was nearing his end, and people came from miles around to be close to him in order to partake of his grace. Unable to bear the pain any longer, he was whisked back to Fonte Colombo, and then across country to Siena to visit more doctors. But his illness now was in its terminal stage. Still alive but already entering into legend, he had become an object of curiosity for many eager to see for themselves the wounds of the Stigmata. One of the brothers, Pacifico, conceived of a plan so that a friend from Brescia might see the wounds on Francis's hands. Because he was now quite blind, Pacifico advised his friend to quietly enter the room and watch when he asked to kiss Francis's hands. "When he offers them to me," he added, "I'll give you a wink and you can come and look." Ghoulish perhaps? Veneration often makes people do things that otherwise might be considered in bad taste.

During medieval times there had always been a market for saints' relics, alive or dead. The people of Assisi were getting edgy, fearing that Francis might be claimed by the Sienese should he die there. They had already lost the body of their former patron, a certain Saint Crispaldo, allegedly a disciple of Saint Peter, who had been stolen by raiders from Bettona. Word was sent out to

Brother Elias, then the Vicar General of the order at Portiuncula, to bring Francis back before it was too late. Elias hurried to Siena and gathered up the wreck of his old friend, before transporting him on a litter to the monastery of Le Celle, outside the walls of Cortona. He and Francis had founded the hermitage in 1211, so the place was familiar to them both. But even here he was not immune from the demands of his native city. Assisi was clamoring for the return of their potential saint. The whiff of a new industry was in the air.

Loaded onto a horse, the poor man was dragged back to Portiuncula to die. His illness was now so bad that he had been reduced to a skeleton. With Perugia threatening to carry off his body, and the people of Assisi growing more vociferous in their demands, it was decided to move Francis yet again, this time to the bishop's palace in the city itself. There he lay down to die. His doctor, however, a certain Buongiovanni from Arezzo, told him that he would live another six weeks or so—"to the end of September or early October." Francis accepted his prognosis calmly, almost joyfully. "Welcome, Sister Death," he said after the doctor's announcement. He further requested that the brothers keep vigil by his bedside singing his favorite poem, the *Canticle of Brother Sun*. It seems he couldn't get enough of his own words. Brother Elias remonstrated with him on the issue of his levity about his coming death, claiming that people in the city expected him to be more dignified. But Francis refused to be parted from his song.

Finally, Francis was transferred back to Portiuncula because he wanted to be close to his beloved Santa Maria degli Angeli Chapel. I think also that he was growing tired of the incessant pressure to die that the city fathers were putting upon him. They wanted to bury him in state, they wanted his bones. Already, I suspect, they were envisaging a great basilica built in his honor from which the city might ultimately benefit. All he desired to do was to allow his blackened body to bear its pain with a little dignity, knowing that once he'd gone others would claim it as their own. Macabre as it sounds, one has to understand the fervor that surrounded his imminent demise. Conscious that he was about to become a permanent relic, Francis sought to cling to life a little longer for the sake of his own *amour propre*. He knew, as no one else did, that eternity grows smaller once you depart the body.

Today, of course, it is hard to imagine the situation he found himself in during those last hours. Santa Maria degli Angeli is a vast baroque edifice surrounded by a thriving city below Assisi. There is no sense here of a simple compound of huts where the first brothers lived. An aura of industry now surrounds the name of Francis, making it almost impossible to comprehend how a man's death could have been regarded with such anticipation. Walking about the piazza in front of the church, I found myself asking why the memory of such a simple man would have been preserved in the guise of such triumphant architecture. It has always puzzled me why Christianity, more than perhaps any other religion, has felt the need to bury its message in such munificent edifices. Christ was no imperialist; yet his followers have made it their business to crucify him on the cross of extravagance.

Francis's death was a public event. The city knew that he was close to it; the brothers at Portiuncula expected it; the Poor Clares at San Damiano awaited it with the same trepidation that they might the first snows of winter. A certain coldness would inevitably overcome the world. Umbria, this land so steeped in mysticism and the sweet remorse of knowing that sadness is not a permanent condition of the heart, awaited the inevitability of his remains being interred in its soft earth. Every avenue of pines and olive grove sought to extend its shade over his memory. He was a product of its soil. He was its precious seed that had remained forever enclosed in its husk.

I think that people felt strongly about Francis's death not because it closed a chapter in the history of the region, but because it began a new one. Spirit is a fragile thing that manifests itself only rarely, and without recourse to either expectation or demand. You can't just will a saint into existence, nor celebrate what he might stand for in the absence of that slow gestation of sensibility around him. This is the key to the appearance in the world of men like Francis. He was born out of a need of people unhappy with their predicament. The world that they knew had distanced them from the primal ground of collective memory. What they missed was the opportunity to re-affirm what exists outside time, as well as within the context of their own lives. For them, spirit was a food more nourishing than any meal.

These are the issues that make Francis's death so poignant and so relevant. He didn't just threaten to pass away, but rather he managed to instill the event with his own powerful sense of the drama of an unfolding metaphysical event. It wasn't just his body and personality that was about to become redundant, but the lingering fear on the part of most that such spirituality might not appear on earth again. He, I think, was aware of these fears, hence the prolongation of his last days. All his actions were choreographed to ensure that as many people as possible might be infected with his yearning for the Infinite. He wanted people to come away from the pain of his death profoundly invigorated. He wanted them to bear his death within themselves, and so carry the torch forward to another generation.

His last actions were carefully orchestrated. His desire to be transferred back to Portiuncula where it all began, his final letter to Clare where he urged her fledgling order to "live always in fidelity" and to regard fatigue as "precious" in the interest of being crowned "queen in heaven," his insistence on his Canticle being sung in his presence each day, and, finally, the letter he asked to be written to a certain Roman lady, Giocoma di Settisole, requesting her to be with him at his death, all suggest a man interested in consummating his own myth. From the latter, as we already know, he asked her to bring a "cloth the color of ashes to cover my body, candles, a cloth to cover my face, and a small pillow for my head." This she dutifully brought, some say miraculously, because she arrived before his letter was sent. As well, Signora Settisole brought him his favorite honey and almond cake that he nibbled on with relish.[2]

Can we not argue that these actions are those of a man concerned about his final moments, and the effect they might have on others? There is talk that he insisted on being taken outside so that he might lie on the ground to die. It is a bizarre request if it is true. At dusk an exaltation of larks flew down very low over the place where he lay. I am reminded of an occasion when I attended the death of an old Aborigine in the Australian desert. There, while the priest performed the burial rites, a huge black crow sat in a nearby tree observing the proceedings with an interested eye. My gaze kept drifting towards this bird, wondering whether it were not an incarnation of the dead man's spirit. Somehow I knew that nature partook of this death, just as the larks may have of Francis's.

Francis lingered on until the evening of October 3, 1226. He was partly conscious, even if unable to speak. While the brothers chanted the psalm *Voce me ad Dominum Clamavi*, he lay on the bare earth, his body true to the spirit of poverty that had formed him. One can only imagine what went through his thoughts during those hours. Did he recall taking off his clothes in Assisi's

---

✳ ————————

2. Giocoma di Settisole, a noble Roman woman, was the widow of a prominent legislator in that city, Graziani Frangipani. She had somehow "earned the privilege of special love" from Francis. Little is known of their relationship, but clearly it was different to the one he had with Clare. Reputedly, Signora Settisole belonged to a lay order founded by Francis for people prevented by their lives to enter the monastic orders. They practiced a simplified form of the Rule "in the world." Today, her remains rest in the crypt in the lower church of San Francesco, near those of Francis.

square? Did he remember selling his father's goods in Foligno to finance his dream of rebuilding the house of God? Had he any recollection of those long, intense conversations with Clare, urging her to break with her life and join him in his? Did any words of his conversation with the sages of Egypt linger in memory? And what of La Verna: would those wounds ever make up for the ecstasy he'd experienced when the seraph visited him? It is hard to say. But such was the intensity of his life that I feel sure that Francis held onto each moment with the joy of a passing spring blossom.

In the end death was the final act in his extraordinary life. He had wrought from the unpromising material of a merchant's son living in a provincial Italian city an existence that can only be likened to that of genius. By upsetting all values pertaining to his societal and personal self Francis had managed to create a new type of being beholden only to the hidden laws of existence. He gave new meaning to these laws by associating them with God's name and with the life of his son, Christ. By choosing to live out the Crucifixion as something other than a historical reality, Francis changed the relationship practicing Christians might have with their Maker. Now they had no choice but to learn how to endure Deity's anguish in themselves as a result of their own falling away from being. The onus was on them to create order, a spiritual order, out of the chaos caused by Christ's death.

Francis's asceticism was the only way he knew how to break the nexus between flesh and its love affair with the illusory. He saw clearly that the death of the senses prefigured an entirely different level of perception. While he had done no more than Saint Anthony and Saint Paul in this respect, or many other anchorites of the Egyptian desert, he had added a dimension to their practices that they had previously ignored. He had placed it at the center of a person's life in this world, not in some remote cave on Mount Colzim or in the Nitria Desert. I don't think Francis wanted men and women to leave this world, to break with their traditions or to destroy the fabric of society itself. He saw no purpose in everyone dismantling their identities in pursuit of some illusory nirvana. This he felt was an exceptional gift that could only be bestowed historically rather than personally. That he had received it was immaterial to the broader spiritual responsibilities to which each person was heir.

Francis had another object in mind when he proposed poverty, chastity, and obedience as the values by which a person might live. Though he never publicly acknowledged it himself, I think he would have recognized that this trinity of values must be seen as the basis for a complete break with the past and with its penchant for historicizing reality. What he wanted to see was its spiritualization so that it might release new energies into the world. Not only had Western man reached an impasse, and was preparing to grovel at the feet of a material order once more, but he had forgotten what it was that had made him so special in the first place: his ability to imagine a world larger and more complete than his own. Such was the landscape that Francis tried to reveal to his contemporaries.

His asceticism had always been a part of the shock treatment that he administered to himself. Those who might have viewed it as part of his sexual *angst*, or a wish to deny the body a role in the growing mercantilization of medieval society, or indeed that in scourging the body he was scourging society itself, these people would be making the mistake of attaching too much importance to the physical aspect of his behavior. I now realize that this was just another act of inversion on his part. He wanted to turn people upside down in relation to the way they perceived themselves. He saw the world (nature) as an eternal act of self-revelation, and man's role in it as its interpreter, not its exploiter. For someone like himself, who had discovered what true freedom was, it was only natural that he should want to make everything in its image, to spread it throughout the entire universe. Asceticism for him was a way of achieving such a conversion; it cleansed reality of its tendency to express material values only.[3]

So he lay there on his rush mat, dying a death that was like no other. It was the German poet Rainer Maria Rilke who said that each man carries within him the style of death he will eventually enact. Certainly Francis perfectly embodied his own. While the populace gathered nearby, eager to catch a glimpse of his Stigmata when he was eventually carried away for burial, while the nuns at San Damiano prayed for his soul, while Clare sat in her cell contemplating the moment when he might quit her thoughts altogether, while Giocoma di Settisole, that Roman lady of mysterious consequence sat by him and caressed his forehead, and while his brethren gathered around singing psalms, this withered homunculus of a man, this hollowed-out cavity of thought, this adversary of the ordinary lay in a state of painful repose, his muscles slowly tightening about his stricken body. Not even at the end did the rack release him from its grip.

Knowing him as I do, and standing in the busy thoroughfare outside the portal of Santa Maria degli Angeli, I am reluctant to enter. His spirit no longer inhabits the dry ground underneath its foundations. Nor have stone and mortar in any way enhanced his presence or conjured up that voice of his, so mellifluous with consequence. Who can hear him above the din of traffic or the sound of bells pealing in his absence? I can. I can hear him exhorting his followers to be strong in their commitment to the spiritual life. He didn't want them to be theologians or bishops or even priests. He simply wanted them to practice a kind of yearning, and to be satisfied with occupying the same penumbra as the mysteries themselves. He knew it was impossible to know Deity.

---

3. Francis liked to quote 1 Corinthians (2:14) in this respect: "the sensual man does not perceive the things of God." He also believed that reverence moves us in a way that ordinary will or consciousness doesn't.

He knew that any man who sought to escape himself was doomed to failure. But most of all, he knew that while the apparent world exists in all its wonder and multiplicity, such was not the true world.

It is strange, knowing that he died within yards of where I stand, that here lay a man who set out to change the way history was perceived. Something inside him rebelled against the relentless nature of causality, even when he knew that this was how the apparent world revealed itself. Deep in his heart, Francis had experienced an epiphany that had taught him how to avoid causality as a means of expressing how he felt. Perhaps he understood it to be the law of the seraph—who knows? I only know that when one visits La Verna another kind of causality takes over. It is a causality that suggests a link between fire and language, between words and their combustible nature. Few people understand why words and flame are linked, except those who are determined to rekindle the lost warmth of the spirit. Francis might have frozen to death had he not discovered the incandescence and unbridled heat of his poetic instinct.

For it is true that after Christ spoke to Francis through the wings of the seraph, he was "overcome by a most intense ardor and flame of divine love," so the *Third Consideration of the Holy Stigmata* tells us. We know also that the Christ Crucified he experienced on the mountain that day "enkindled his mind." It was suggested, too, that "all of Mount La Verna seemed on fire with very bright flames" on that fateful morning. We can already begin to sense what Francis might have experienced. What did it all mean, one might ask? Francis had always been reluctant to speak of the event save to inform a few of his companions that "this great mystery is reserved for the future." So now we know: the Crucifixion was not an historic event, but a spiritual one. It partook of the totality of the divine powers and emanations embodied in the idea of Christ as the representative on earth of Deity's fullness.

Even on that spring morning I couldn't help feeling how lucky I was to have walked in the footsteps of Francis. To have trekked the back roads and cobbled lanes of Umbria in his wake was to have experienced a spirituality that I was unfamiliar with. His was that of *cogitio matutina*, the morning knowledge, the deep interpenetration of supernatural reality with its counterpart in the world. As a practitioner of Illuminism, he understood more than most how to break down the barrier between the two so that a fruitful cross-fertilization might occur. Traveling throughout Umbria, I had found myself entering a landscape that was both visionary yet real at the same time.

On the night of his death Portiuncula became a node of pain wedded to a palpable sense of release. Francis's brethren stood vigil beside him, along with Giocoma di Settisole. Insisting that he again be laid on the ground outside, Francis asked his friends to remove his sackcloth so that he might be naked once more. Then, placing his left hand over the wound in the upper part of his right side out of a sense of modesty, he raised one hand to the heavens and made his final pronouncement: "It is enough. I have done what was mine to do. May Christ teach all of you what you must do." Men sobbed. His guardian, who understood how Francis felt at this moment, advised him that his sackcloth belonged to him, not to Francis, and that he would reclaim it after his death. Francis smiled. Lady Poverty had stood by him to the end. He was dying in the state that he had been born into.

Everything about Francis's death spoke of his lifelong commitment to simplicity. He had proved that it was possible to dispense with the normal structures of living, and to forge new ones in the fire of trust. Poverty was not a condition of lack for him, but a philosophy. No, it was more than that—because buried in the word itself was his true mistress: poetry. He had tried to live a poetic life, a life steeped in the mystery of words drifting like butterflies over the landscape of human experience. More than most, he had learned how to recognize the patterns that words create, and how these patterns contain the celestial version of consciousness to which he had always aspired.

His death nearly eight hundred years ago is still vivid. Something about the man hasn't yet died. Even when his body was carried up to San Damiano by the brethren on its way to Assisi for burial in the church of St. George, one senses that he still had gifts to bestow. Clare waited for him behind the bars of her monastery, her love for him still as fervent as ever. Not even death could silence their yearning for God through one another. To the sound of hymns and the psalm *Voce me ad Dominum clamavi*, the brothers and clergy raised his limp body on outstretched hands so that Clare might gaze upon her great love through the open grille for the last time. His eyes, deep-set and dark, were closed. His wounds, it seemed, were healed. The seraph had made its final utterance. Their leave-taking was over; Clare slowly shut her grille, and the cortege moved on up the hill in the morning sunlight.

CHAPTER TWELVE

The Path
of the Rose

✳

I t is often hard to assess a man who lived so far back in time, especially when he has been claimed by millions throughout the world. Francis is one of those uniquely charismatic figures whose light continues to reach us across the centuries. But I have always felt that he has been ill-served by his biographers who always wanted to highlight his Catholicity at the expense of his universality. Now that I have made this journey through his life and his land, I feel that his universality authenticates him more. Francis was both a man of his time and someone who stood for values that transcended his age. He was born at a moment when society was undergoing profound change. Medieval life and the reign of feudalism were entering their last phase: the individual was about to burst forth and blossom as Europe's new exemplar.

Francis absorbed these tensions like the proverbial lightning rod that he was. He never questioned his feudal allegiance when it came to acknowledging the Church of Rome's right to oversee how its followers believed. The principle of hierarchy stemming from God through his vicar on earth was entirely acceptable to him. But when it came to the more personal nature of spirituality, Francis never hesitated in taking the lead. As far as he was concerned, a man must take charge of his own spiritual destiny and forge it into an instrument worthy of the battle at hand. Few before him had seen life as so precious that it could be abandoned in the service of an ideal higher than himself. Alone among men and women, he gave his life away rather than subject it to the constraints that he felt fear might impose.

I admired him for that. One only has to visit the places that he called home to realize how easy it was for him to pack his bag and move on. If he ever had a bag, of course! His sense of absolute independence from things, from bodily support, shines forth from everything he did and thought. If he did have any possessions, then these were both intellectual and spiritual, and so far more valuable. He had finally learned how to exist in the world by making as few demands on it as might be required to sustain life. His body worked in accordance with the laws of nature. In many ways, he was closer to the Neolithic figures depicted in the Altamira caves of Spain than he was to the people of Umbria. He craved an inner wildness of spirit more than he did the stolidity inherent in belonging somewhere. Francis made it possible for those who came after him to choose exile as their hidden territory of growth. It's no accident that the greatest names of the Renaissance did their best work away from their native soil. Men such as Dante, Leonardo da Vinci, Michelangelo, and Raphael join an earlier group of wanderers throughout Europe—those medieval translators of Toledo and Palermo who journeyed from as far north as England to pursue their vocation in the south. I'm thinking of men like Adelard of Bath, Robert of Chestor, and Gerard of Cremona who spent their lives engaged in translating Arabic texts in foreign lands.

In today's world of affluence it is equally hard to understand why a man might choose poverty as his credo. Let's face it, moreness rather lessness is an undisputed article of faith for most of us. Such is our addiction to things that we find it difficult to know how poverty could prove to be so attractive. But I think this misses the point. Poverty is *not* attractive, hence its fascination for such a gifted inverter like Francis. He wanted to prove that which may appear to be of negative value in the realization of human consciousness, is in fact a mark of ethical maturity. To renounce what one perhaps aspires to both early, and naturally, as Francis had so clearly done, is to abandon what Eckhart called "world-historical magnitudes." He simply gave up the fight to be a person in the way it is normally understood. If he were alive today, I'm quite sure he would refuse to belong to a health maintenance organization, or put himself down for unemployment benefits, or pay into the tax agency's coffers. The Francis that I have come to know and respect would see these acts as belonging to the predication of fear that underpins modern society and its yearnings.

In this sense I believe that Francis is both medieval and modern. No benefits drawn from an elaborate education could have made him more aware of the underlying conflicts of his age. He saw through its desire to concentrate power and wealth in the hands of the privileged few, while maintaining a veneer of piety to prop up a crumbling edifice. Worldly popes and sacrilegious kings continued to empty the age of its timeless wisdom and spiritual heritage. The lower classes too had grown venal in pursuit of their small share of the newly created wealth generated in such cities as Florence, Perugia, Pisa, and Venice. Probably Francis had seen this phenomenon on a wider scale when he perhaps traveled throughout Europe in his father's company during his early years. He may well have witnessed merchants squeezing deals out of poverty-stricken craftsmen to their own advantage. Sacks of gold, carts laden with articles of trade crossing the Alps, and military escorts all went hand in hand. Greed and the sword were now cohorts.

Is it any wonder that Francis chose a life that scorned privilege or the benefits of office? He neither wanted to be a successful merchant, nor later even a priest. He despised commerce because it exploited man's acquisitive instincts, just as he distanced himself from pursuing a life in the Church, and so exercising some form of curial authority. He wanted no part of a life that was dedicated to the realization of success, be it monetary or spiritual. He would rather be known as a man who denied success altogether than someone who was beholden to its demands. I think this is one of the secrets of his appeal: Francis spurned secular values even as he suggested new ones.

And what were these values? Reading his work, and the recollections of his biographers, one senses that he had little new to say to his time other than to reaffirm early Christian ideals in the face of increasing secularism. His appeal lay in the fact that he was less than subtle in his desire to return to the spiritual practices of the Desert Fathers. Many people saw in these ideals a clear path that had not been sullied by theology or dogma. They wanted simply to celebrate the Passion of Christ as a seminal event in the history of the world. They liked the idea that the world was a changed place since the advent of Christ. His appearance on earth had caused a hiatus between the old and the new, between the pagan and the Christian. For simple folk, this held considerable appeal since it justified their sense of inclusion.

Francis also renewed people's awareness in the possibility of having a personal relationship with God. Medieval spirituality had tended to emphasize the social implications of religion whereby all people held to the same beliefs. Doctrine was worked out in Rome; the imperial language of Latin encapsulated the liturgy and the Bible in words that were increasingly misunderstood by ordinary folk. The less educated in the community, and they constituted the majority, were thus forced to accept their religion as a given rather than as something that they might actually participate in. Hence the emphasis placed upon church attendance and the many pageants conducted throughout the liturgical year. Belief in the Christian message was no longer a living thing, but instead had become set in rituals that everyone accepted without question.

Francis understood the problem more than most, though not at the conceptual level. I think it was his body that did most of the questioning on his behalf. He used it as his barometer to test the pressure of society's ills. History rarely intimates that medieval society may have been experiencing a spiritual crisis. But when one looks at the suppression of the Cathars in France, the decline of the papacy as a spiritual force throughout Europe, and the way excommunication was summarily wielded by popes against political foes, it's easy to see that the so-called "unity" of medieval society can and ought to be questioned. Nor is it an accident that Giotto painted the life of Francis with the same care for miraculous detail as he might the life of Christ. The two had become synonymous: a carpenter and a merchant's son found themselves embodying heroic virtues of the spirit in the way that no aristocrat or king could do. In Francis, as in Christ, spiritual integrity had been wrested back from the pharisaic culture that sought to use it as the source of its own power.

There was something deeply political about Francis's actions, although he was careful to conceal his motives beneath a cloak of spirituality. I don't believe he did so consciously, nor do I think that he set himself a political agenda. His commitment to the renewal of society was a spontaneous gesture motivated by his desire to make Christian belief the fulcrum of society once more. In this sense, his message was similar to Christ's. His popularity among the common folk was derived from the fact that he did *not* embody theological virtue; but rather, he espoused a mode of living that was clear-cut and relatively simple. Poverty, for him, was an act of self-discipline that could not be interpreted in any other way than as a rebuke to a society already beginning to distance itself from the rigors of a hardly won survival.

His appearance in Umbria and Tuscany as a wandering mendicant who made beggary into a compact between almsgiver and beggar should not pass unnoticed. Until his arrival mendicants begged so that they might eat, and because they had no money. Francis made beggary into a statement about the virtue of poverty, and so enlisted the sentiments of those who gave. He wanted the almsgiver to understand why he was giving, and why the mendicant chose hunger as his staff. In his hands, food became a statement about the right of everyone to eat, no matter what their status might be. Hunger, not economics, must constitute the benchmark by which a person's right to life might be judged. No other figure since Christ had truly understood the link between nourishment and virtue—that food, or the lack of it, was essentially the stuff that made spiritual renewal possible.[1]

For this reason Francis refused to allow money to enter his possession. He knew better than most that money removes from any act of exchange the spiritual gift that giving embodies. Unlike food, money is a neutral object, something abstract, the result of men wanting to remove the emotion inherent in food, and so to facilitate exchange at a more rational level. Money is a method of exchange that precludes the idea of poverty, since to have it (on either side of the exchange, that is) implies the neutralization of poverty. Francis instinctively knew this, hence his

---

✳ ──────────

1. The *Little Flowers of Saint Francis*, an anonymous contemporary text, stated his views on poverty with clarity and precision: "The treasure of blessed poverty is so very precious and divine that we are not worthy to possess it in our vile bodies. For poverty is that heavenly virtue by which all earthly and transitory things are trodden underfoot, and by which every obstacle is removed from the soul, so that it might freely enter into union with the eternal Lord God. It is also the virtue which makes the soul, while still here on earth, converse with the angels in Heaven."

edicts against the brothers having any contact with money. We understand now why he asked one of his friars to pick up the coins with his mouth and place them in the ass's dung outside. What he feared most was the contamination that possessing money might inflict on a mind less able to recognize the virtue of poverty for its own sake.

His actions, as bizarre as they may seem at first encounter, are not so when analyzed carefully. I have suggested earlier that I believed that Francis was a master of the shock effect. He understood that people could only be brought to their senses by some irrational gesture capable of dismantling normal patterns of thought. I am reminded of the Zen priest subjecting his pupils to a *koan*, and the necessity of understanding the irrational nature of the riddle. Francis used gesture and action to effect a similar conclusion. Who cannot forget how he asked his friend Brother Masseo to decide on what road to take—either to Siena, Florence, or to Arezzo—by turning around and around until dizziness overcame him? What Francis wanted from his friend was to disassociate himself from the act of making a decision at all, or from willing his next move. He wanted Masseo to "leave his senses" and so put the decision about which direction to take in the hands of God. In this respect, Francis was no different than the Zen priest: both wanted to encourage the birth of will-lessness and irrationalism in the minds of their pupils.

The act of removing one's clothes, of going naked through the streets, of talking to birds and animals, of sleeping in the open and eating scraps from other men's tables, these were none other than the gestures of a man who understood how to shock. He sensed that human beings were basically conservative in their relations with one another—that they rarely, if ever, wanted to engage in acts that might question the advantage of hiding behind good manners for their own sake. I think he knew that too much emphasis on the virtue of politeness led to men and women losing contact with one another, except on the shallowest of levels. He saw better than most that rudeness was important if men were ever going to question their conduct. A man needed to break out of the constraints of conformity that governed his actions. He needed to put aside the old Adam and adopt the robe of nudity in all that he thought or did. It is noticeable that Francis insisted on his friars possessing only one tunic to clothe their bodies. He wanted them always to feel that they were *once removed* from the state into which they were born. Innocence, it seems, was closely aligned with that of having few manners, and almost no clothes.

In contrast to this rather revolutionary behavior Francis insisted on obedience that, on the surface, appears to reinforce the medieval principle of hierarchy and social conformity. In many ways, it did. But in another way, the obedience he espoused was one of spiritual obedience to a higher cause rather than that to either Church or state. Even to suggest an obedience to God that was above the Church is an interesting departure from feudalism. If one considers that the Church overreached the state, which in turn overreached the individual, then the idea that the individual might bypass both in order to establish a direct contact with God, is a marked indication of a shift in emphasis. The Stigmata, clearly, is both a miraculous event and a political statement: in the history of the Church few men and women had received their spiritual imprimatur directly from God. It had always come to them via the Church. Sainthood was recognized as the Church's way of paying homage to the excellence of one of its flock. But in Francis's case, this recognition had come directly from God via the seraph. Obedience for him never truly entailed the acknowledgment of human authority; his was directed to God alone. His relationship with the Church in Rome, therefore, was always going to be paradoxical. To be a fool for God was one thing, but to carry this over into a wholesale rejection of curial authority would have placed him, at least potentially, at the mercy of inquisitors.

He must have surely heard what was going on in Aquitaine with the suppression of the Cathars. Moreover, their stronghold of Montségur was destroyed in 1244 by the Roman Catholic armies led by Simon de Montfort, a liegeman to the French king, only a few years after his own death. Religious suppression was on the rise throughout Europe.[2]

Finally, there was his vow of chastity. I have said much on this subject earlier, but feel that one point needs to be added. Chastity is the ultimate act of detachment from society because it negates its very premise. People rarely see how revolutionary chastity can be a gesture of noncompliance. Too often we get bogged down in the sexual aspect of the issue without considering its social effects. Chastity revokes the human condition and its perpetual round of birth and death and birth again. It asks of men and women to abandon their commitment to what the Buddhists regard as our karmic condition. Jacopone da Todi (1230–1306), himself very much a Franciscan, called chastity a "fair flower of long-stemmed Love" and a "fortress that guards a great treasure." Francis would have agreed. He knew that only a soul bedecked in chastity could slowly move toward God's Spouse, none other than the Virgin of Purity. Chastity alone freed men and women from social constraints in order to pursue this course.

Francis was the first person to articulate his values as both being political and ascetic. We know that initially he had no desire to set up an order, only to establish a rule by which brothers might live. He saw his virtues as a bulwark against the materialism and corruption of his age. If they were there merely to reinforce the constitution of his order, then they would have been

---

✳ ─────────

2. Simon de Montfort, a loyal Catholic, destroyed the fortress of Minerve in southwest France in 1210. This was just one battle in what is known as the Albigensien Crusade. Francis would have been most conscious of the danger of going it alone in his spiritual quest. The Cathars had learned this to their cost, and he would have been aware of what they had paid.

shorn of any revolutionary effect. Francis wanted his brothers to remain totally outside established institutions, which he saw as little more than halfway houses that considered the pursuit of Christian belief without the benefit of their guidance as dangerous, even heretical. He knew, as Christ had known, that one must die completely to the world in order to achieve everlasting life. But he was also conscious that "everlasting life" was no panacea for the living. It must be an interior acquisition, not a sojourn in some heavenly domain. In his last testament, written in the bishop's palace a few months prior to his death, Francis mentioned Heaven only once and in passing. He was more conscious of stressing the importance of receiving the blessings of "His beloved Son" on this earth rather than those in the next life. He was more interested in the blessings that might accrue to a person after the elimination of self through a lifetime of asceticism than he was worrying about what might occur after his "second death."

At a personal level, we can identify with Francis more than we might with other saints. It is because his vocation sprang from a deeply felt human affliction rather than some immediate revelation. We know that he underwent a long period of doubt and conflict that forced him to wander down a number of blind alleys before he actually understood what was expected of him. We know that he had no one to turn to, no guide or confidant or confessor that might help him arrive at his decision to quit the world. One forgets that his decision was reached in the privacy of his own thoughts. He served no novitiate; no priest or abbot guided him; he had none of the support that a monastery might offer him as he moved toward his conversion. Francis acted alone. He made himself into his own spiritual lodestone. This strikes a chord with many of us today as we try to negotiate for ourselves a genuine inner life not necessarily sanctioned by one philosophy or religion. He wanted to find out for himself how and what to believe—and, moreover, how to realize his goal of imitating Christ.

In this sense, Francis is extremely modern. Unlike others of his age he wanted to take control of his own spiritual life. That he clearly aligned himself with the Church does not negate his bid to create a spirituality based upon the principles of early Christianity, rather than those of institutional religion itself. No one was more aware than he as to the risks inherent in intellectualizing spirituality. He wanted his to be simpler, more flexible, less conditioned by doctrine. As far as he was concerned the seraph could only be approached by way of a pure heart, not that of systematic knowledge. His religion was a religion of the heart.

Which brings us to consider his relationship with people. There's no doubt that he was capable of inspiring undying loyalty and love. Few, if any of his followers denounced him as a charlatan, or left his side during his life. Since the day he entered the order in 1210, Brother Leo hardly let the man out of his sight. Clare never forgot the impression he made on her when she was a young woman, nor did Brother Elias, the consummate administrator, politician, and dilettante, fail to heed his call at the last and bring him to Cortona. The brilliant Anthony of Padua never doubted that Francis was right when he cautioned him against learning. Kings and popes acknowledged his gifts, and defended him against those who might wish to dilute his message. Even the sages of Egypt had no doubt in their minds that they were dealing with an exceptional man who radiated a love of humanity.

But his love was not a personal love as we might understand it. Rather, he had detached himself from the preoccupations of gender and personality in his bid to reach out to the soul of a person. He knew, as few would have known, that silence allowed for a deeper interpenetration of being than that of mere affection. Clare understood this, too. Though she may have felt a desire to possess him in her youth, clearly this feeling passed in time.

Like the god Hermes, whose symbol is mercury, Francis could not be contained by the normal constraints of affection or friendship. He slipped through the fingers of possession. The only occasion when his capacity for unconditional love might have been tested was in his relations with his parents. But I harbor a sneaking suspicion that this benighted couple remained in his thoughts, however difficult their initial disagreements might have been. I cannot believe that his father did not finally recognize the sincerity of his son's vocation once he had witnessed his effect upon most of his countrymen. Bernardone may have been a worldly man, but he was no fool. I suspect he secretly admired his son for bridging the gap between his own unorthodox sympathies and the demands of a more conventional spirituality.

What Francis bestowed upon the spiritual conditions of his time was something altogether refreshing. Though he was a serious man in himself, and never relented from subjecting himself to a most rigorous ascetical discipline, we know from the records that he was lighthearted, that he enjoyed life, that he never allowed himself to be dragged down by his physical sufferings. The soul of the poet reigned in him. I am reminded of his sense of play in his dealing with Brother Masseo, a tall, good-looking brother whose success as a beggar was better than most. The story is worth repeating, as it sums up the way Francis inspired those about him with his unexpected and wholly unconventional behavior.

WHEN THEY CAME to a certain church, Francis said to his companion: "Let's go in and hear Mass, and pray there." They entered, but as the priest was absent Francis went and hid himself behind the altar to pray. While he was praying there, he was granted a divine vision which wholly inflamed him with such an intense longing and love for holy poverty that flames of love seemed to issue from his face and mouth.

Going out to his companion, all afire with love, he said force-
fully: "Aha! Aha! Aha! Brother Masseo, give yourself to me!"

He said it three times. Amazed at his fervor, Brother Masseo
threw himself into the holy Father's arms when he said to
him: "Give yourself to me!"

Then Francis, with his mouth open wide, and repeating very
loudly "Aha! Aha! Aha!," by the power of the Holy Spirit
lifted Brother Masseo up in the air with his breath, and pro-
jected him forward the length of a long spear throw.

Brother Masseo was completely astounded. He later told his
companions that he had experienced such spiritual conso-
lation and sweetness in being raised up and projected by
the breath of Francis that he did not recall ever having had
such a great consolation in all his life.

✳

It is a remarkable story for a number of reasons. Firstly, we are
again alerted to Francis's indifference to the formal side of religion. If there was no Mass to be heard that day, this presented no
obstacle to him in his desire to remain in the continued presence
of God. Moreover, he was quite capable of going behind the altar
to pray if it might offer him privacy. Further, and this is significant, he seemed to possess an uncanny ability to know when he
was about to be subjected to an ecstatic experience. He seemed to
will himself into a state of bliss whenever he desired, although
I'm sure it wasn't the case. Whatever the truth might be, Francis
somehow knew when was the right moment to exercise his paranormal powers.

Again we encounter the power of breath. Uttering the expression "Aha! Aha! Aha!" numerous times is no ordinary gesture of
exuberance. Many Sufi orders today use such a rapid expulsion

of breath to generate a feeling of ecstasy when they are perform-
ing the *dhikr*. I have experienced precisely the same thing among
the Mevlana Sufis in Istanbul. At the height of their slow gyration
about the room, each man cries out "Aha! Aha! Aha!" in rapid
fashion. The sudden loss of air, and a subsequent rapid intake,
produces a strange physical effect on almost everyone. They find
themselves elevated, as if slightly drunk; yet at the same time their
minds remain clear. To suggest that one might be "inflamed" or
"afire with love" is no exaggeration. The entire ritual of the *dhikr*
is designed to invoke such an experience.

To have projected Brother Masseo as far as a long spear throw
by his extraordinary utterance (note that his mouth was wide
open, surely an indication of the stress Francis was suffering at
this point: bliss for some might well be an overpowering experience), suggests that he *could not contain* what was inside him. His
spiritual condition was such that he needed to release the energies trapped there. Repeatedly calling to Masseo "Come to me!"
intimates that he may not have known what he was saying, either—or indeed, what he was doing. Language may have been
the only tool at his disposal to initiate a fundamental shift in consciousness, not only for himself but for Masseo. To suggest also
that Masseo wasn't thrown some distance by the power of his
voice, that such practices are no more than psychic projections, is
to fly in the face of innumerable similar recorded events being
performed by yogis in India, by fakirs, and tribal hierophants.
Who has not seen or heard of ecstatics raising great weights under hypnosis, or of fakirs entering into a state of suspended ani-
mation during prolonged periods of entombment? It may be that
Francis did possess unusual psychic powers that were triggered
by spiritual ecstasy.

Which leads us to those events at La Verna. The Stigmata will
always remain with us as one of the most striking spiritual events
in history. No one except skeptics seriously doubts that it occurred.

Contemporary evidence is too strong and too well attested by historians not to confirm that something altogether otherworldly happened on that September morning in 1224. For Francis, it was a culmination of a lifetime of ascetical discipline that was directed, as he so readily admitted, to enabling his soul to converse with angels. He knew what he was doing even if he couldn't anticipate the outcome. The miracle of his life is not that he received the Stigmata, but that his intense desire to imitate Christ in all that he did and suffered was realized in its fullness. Francis achieved his spirit's desire—to be stigmatized, to be wounded in his very being, to take upon himself the sufferings of a dying God in order to affirm their timeless validity. He knew, as no one else before him had done, that Christ's crucifixion was an act of sacrifice directed at God itself. For the God-man needed to suffer for the benefit of His own creation. In this respect, I am reminded of Heraclitus when he observed that "all things come to pass through conflict." Christ knew, as did his disciple Francis, how true this remark was. The "limits of the soul" (Heraclitus) could only be realized when there was a compact, by way of conflict, between God and His progeny.

Francis became a bridge between ancient thought and his day. He made people realize that the soul inhabited psychic territory, and therefore could not be dispelled from the world. His love of nature, and his awareness that all things were alive (including rocks), reached back to the ancient Greek belief in *empsycha*, which maintained that "all things are full of gods" (Thales). To suggest that life emerged from non-life was both irrational and unnatural. Francis believed this also. He knew that the limitlessness of the soul could not be comprehended, or experienced under normal life conditions, that somehow a person must engage in acts of psychic or spiritual vertigo in order to realize his own stigmata. The truth is that for the Stigmata to occur, one must allow oneself to be crucified in accordance with one's own nature. The Stigmata is a manifestation of life's anguish and blessedness that we may all experience it in one way or another.

One shouldn't see Francis's Stigmata solely as the reflection of some religious event. It is far more than that. It is the re-creation of an idea of suffering, and of conflict, that is deeply imbedded in human experience. Any thought of eliminating it from the world is futile, however much we might desire to see an end to conflict and suffering. According to Heraclitus, a wise observer in these matters, Homer was wrong when he wrote: "Would that Conflict might vanish from among gods and men!" Rather, as the philosopher believed, there wouldn't be any "attunement" (harmony) without highs and lows and the nourishment of the opposites (contrasts). The Stigmata reflects a momentary resolution of these opposites, these opposing forces of conflict, before they too fall back into the abyss of Justice, which is none other than the cauldron of existence itself.

I now understood why Francis has become such an attractive figure to me during the course of my journey throughout Italy. He took me back to the very origin of myself. In his company I felt freer than I would have if I had been left to deal solely with the Italy of history and culture. In his own way he didn't represent any civilizing force whatsoever. Whenever I sat in his caves and grottos, or visited the remote monasteries that he had founded, or tramped the forest around La Verna, I always felt that I was in the presence of a much wilder man than the ordinary Italian. He'd tapped a vein of *ecstasis* that the more urbane medieval gentleman barely understood, let alone might have experienced. Was he a primitive? Perhaps. It may be that his early struggles as a young man were mainly confined to dealing with his urbanity and the cultural accretion of nearly fifteen hundred years of Classico-Christian civilization. In order to renew himself he had been forced to break with this tradition altogether.

My journey had brought me to a point where I felt I understood the man at last. He was no longer a pious saint, the founder
of a monastic order, a pillar of the Church; he was someone that
I could identify with in all his sufferings. His confusion and uncertainty, his pain and anguish, his uncertainty and conflict—all
these made sense to me as I struggled to recognize the curve of
my own life. In his own way Francis made me realize how important it was to carry within my thoughts a "Francis of the imagination," someone who transcended the limits imposed on his
memory by history. It seemed to me as I stood in the lamp-lit
crypt of the lower church of the basilica of St. Francis and gazed
up at his rough stone sarcophagus secured by an iron grille, that
I was looking at a different man than I had earlier imagined. He
had become more human. His spirituality was more accessible.
Something about his absence penetrated me deeply. I think he
renewed my faith in the idea that the human adventure was an
act of spiritual recovery, not some voyage after ephemera. I recall
a remark made by Heidegger in this respect when he said that
our role is to be a "shepherd of Being." What he meant, I suspect,
was that we must acquire the essential poverty of a shepherd and
so dwell in the open, free space of a night sky, knowing that above
was a configuration of stars that would always remain incomprehensible yet familiar.

Francis belongs to the whole world, not just to Assisi or the
Church. I walked out of the basilica of San Francesco that morning, knowing that my journey had been a rich one. I had taken
possession of something precious. I had wandered the back roads
of Umbria, inched my way into overgrown crypts, sought solace
in caves as old as Egypt, gazed at worn-out reliquaries in glass
exhibits, sat in darkened churches lit only by a few candles, looked
up at frescoes depicting myriad sacred events, genuflected in front
of icons, sat on the edge of cliffs and surveyed tree-clad valleys
below, attended vespers with monks who regarded solitude as

their harvest, watched children singing hymns, glanced at old women muttering prayers, attended weddings, funerals, and baptisms by accident, talked to old priests, watched nuns disappear down alleys, heard birds announce themselves, and finally listened to the breathtaking beauty of Gregorian song in remote chapels on hilltops. This is the world that Francis invited me to enter as I followed in his footsteps. He had made me privy to a world inspired by his example, and I thanked him for that. What more could I ask of him now than that he remain the Bodhisattva of my dreams, the guru of my waking moments, the saint that inhabited my solitude? Yes, there was one more demand that I could make: I could ask him to remain the living icon of an intense humanness that we all aspire to make our own.

Select Bibliography

Abulafia, David. *Frederick II: A Medieval Emperor.* London: Penguin, 1988.

Affifi, A. E. *The Mystical Philosophy of Muhyid Din-Ibnul Arabi.* Lahore: Sh. Muhammad Ashraf, 1964.

Athanasius, Saint. *The Life of Antony and the Letter to Marcellinus;* translation and introduction by Robert C. Gregg. New York: Paulist Press, 1980.

Asín Palacios, Miguel. *La Escatología musulmana en la Divina Comedia: seguida de la historia y crítica de una polémica.* Madrid: Editorial Maestre, 1961.

Bargellini, Piero. *The Little Flowers of Saint Clare,* Edizioni Porziuncola, 1997.

Burckhardt, Jacob. *The Civilization of the Renaissance in Italy.* Vienna, The Phaidon Press, 1937.

Bonaventure, Saint. *The Life of St. Francis.* New York: Paulist Press, 1998.

Butler, Salvator, O.F.M., ed. *We Were With St. Francis,* translated from the Latin text published in *I fiori dei tre compagni* by Jacques Cambell, O.F.M. Chicago: Franciscan Herald Press, 1976.

Brady, Ignatius, O.F.M. *The Writings of St. Francis.* Translated from the *Actus Beati Francisci et Sociorum.* Editioni Porziuncola, 1995.

Campbell Ross, Ian. *Umbria: A Tour Through its History, Landscape, Architecture.* Penguin, 1996.

Chesterton, G. K. *St. Francis of Assisi,* Garden City, N.Y.: Image Books, 1957, 1924.

Corbin, Henry. *Creative Imagination in the Sufism of Ibn Arabi,* translated from the French by Ralph Manheim. Princeton University Press, 1969.

Coulton, G. G. *Medieval Panorama,* New York: Norton, 1974.

Dante Alighieri, *The Comedy of Dante Alighieri, the* Florentine; translated by Dorothy L Sayers. 3 vols. Baltimore: Penguin Books, 1949.

Degl'Innocenti Gambuti, Marcella. *I codici miniati medievali della Biblioteca communale e dell'Accademia etrusca di Cortona.* Firenze: S.P.E.S., 1977.

Dronke, Peter. *The Medieval Lyric,* London: Hutchinson, 1978.

Eco, Umberto. *Art and Beauty in the Middle Ages,* New Haven: Yale University Press, 1986.

Evans, Joan, ed. *The Flowering of the Middle Ages.* London: Thames & Hudson, 1966.

Freccero, John. *Dante: A Collection of Critical Essays.* Englewood Cliffs, N. J., Prentice-Hall, 1965.

Giotto, Great Painters series. New York: William Farquar Payson, 1931.

Green, Julien. *God's Fool,* translated by Peter Heinegg. San Francisco: Harper & Row, 1987, 1985.

Haskins, Charles H. *Studies in the History of Medieval Science,* Cambridge: Harvard University Press, 1927.

Hibbert, Christopher. *The Rise and Fall of the House of Medici*, London: Allen Lane, 1974.

Heidegger, Martin. *Discourse on Thinking*, translated by John M. Anderson and E. Hans Freund. New York: Harper & Tow, 1966.

Ibn Arabi. *A Collection of Mystical Odes From Ibn Arabi*, translated by R. A. Nicholson.

Jacopone, da Todi. *The Lauds*. New York: Paulist Press, 1982.

Kierkegaard, Søren. *Concluding Unscientific Postscript*, translated by David F. Swenson. Princeton: Princeton University Press, 1941.

Lainati, Sister Chiara Augusta, O.S.C. *Saint Clare of Assisi.*, Editioni Porziuncola, 1994.

Le Roy Ladurie, Emmanuel. *Montaillou: Cathars and Catholics in a French Village, 1294–1324.* London: Penguin Books, 1980, 1978.

Little Flowers of Saint Francis, New York: New American Library, 1964.

Moorman J. R. H. *The Sources for the Life of St. Francis of Assisi*, Manchester: Manchester University Press, 1940.

Panofsky, Erwin. *Studies in Iconography: Humanistic Themes in the Art of the Renaissance*. New York: Harper & Row, 1962. Picard, Marc, O.F.M. Cap. *L'Icone du Christ de Saint Damien*, Casa Editrice Francescana, 1989.

Pirenne, Henri. *Medieval Cities: Their Origins and the Revival of Trade*. New York: Doubleday, 1956.

Power, Eileen. *Medieval People*, London: Methuen, 1963.

Robinson, James M., ed. *The Nag Hammadi Library*. San Francisco: Harper C & Row, 1990.

Runciman, Steven. *A History of the Crusades*. 3 vols. Cambridge University Press, 1951–1954.

___. *The Medieval Manichee: A Study of the Christian Dualist Heresy*. Cambridge University Press, 1982.

___. *The Eastern Schism: A Study of the Papacy and the Eastern Churches*. New York: AMS Press, 1983, 1955.

Rumi, Jalalludin. *A Selection of Odes from the Divan of Shems of Tabriz*, translated by James Cowan. Element Books, 1995.

Sarton, George. *A Guide to the History of Science.* Waltham, Mass: Chronica Botanica, 1952.

Southern, R. W. *The Making of the Middle Ages.* New Haven: Yale University Press, 1965.

Southern. R. W. *Medieval Humanism*. New York: Harper & Row, 1970.

Shah, Idries. *The Sufis*. Garden City, N. Y.: Anchor Books, 1971.

Suhrawardi, Shihabuddin. *The Mystical and Visionary Treatises*, translated by W. M. Thackston. Octagon Press, 1982.

The Shrine of La Verna. Arti Grafiche B.N. Marconi, Genova.

Thomas of Aquinas, Saint. *Philosophical Texts*; selected and translated with notes and an introduction by Thomas Gilby. Durham, N. C.: Labyrinth Press, 1982.

Thomas of Celano. *St. Francis of Assisi: First and Second Life With Selections From the Treatise on the Miracles of Blessed Francis*. Assisi: Editrice Minerva, 1996.

Thomas of Celano. *The Life of St. Clair Virgin*. Assisi: Editrice Minerva, 1996.

Tufail, Abu Bakh Muhammad, *The Journey of a Soul: the Story of Hai bin Yaqzan*, translated by Raid Kocasche. Octagon Press, 1985.

Waddell, Helen. *The Wandering Scholars*. New York: Barnes & Noble, 1968.

Wilkinson, John, ed. *Jerusalem Pilgrimage 1099-1185*. Hakluyt Society, 1988

Watt. W. M. *The Influence of Islam on Medieval Europe*, Edinburgh: University Press, 1972.